DAVID'S MIGHTY MEN

Greetings!

First, thank you so much for picking up this book. I hope it's as much fun for you to read as it was for me to create. *David's Mighty Men* is a very important project to me personally, something born out of my desire to encourage young people to be all they can be.

You see, I am a big fan of "heroes". Not of any specific ones, necessarily. I like the "idea" of heroes. To me a hero is someone who works to be their personal best. They sacrifice time and energy, hewing their skills and talents, but not for personal gain or glory. They work hard so they can better serve others. To me, that's a hero.

When I was a child, that's what attracted me to heroic characters, whether in film, books, or comics. It's why I got into the comic business. All these fantastic characters, daily sacrificing, just to help others in their time of need. If you needed help, you could count on them. There is a magic and a wonder in that. More importantly, there is a hope in that. A hope that tells us, "You're not alone in this." "Someone is watching." "Someone cares." "Someone is ready to save you."

I believe everyone needs to know that, no matter how young or old you are. I also believe children need to know something even more important: you don't have to settle for being the helpless victim. You can be the hero! *David's Mighty Men* is about people who are heroes... just like you. Ordinary people (well, okay, maybe not so ordinary), flaws and all, who decide to trust in something bigger than themselves to help them conquer whatever obstacles might get in the way. After all, "heroes" need help too!

Saddle up your horses, this is going to be a great adventure.

Sincerely yours,

Javier Saltares

P.S. -- This book is dedicated to my wife Robyn and our three children, Travis, Matthew, and Sarah, who believed in me when I didn't believe in myself.

www.dmmcomics.com
www.communitycomics.com

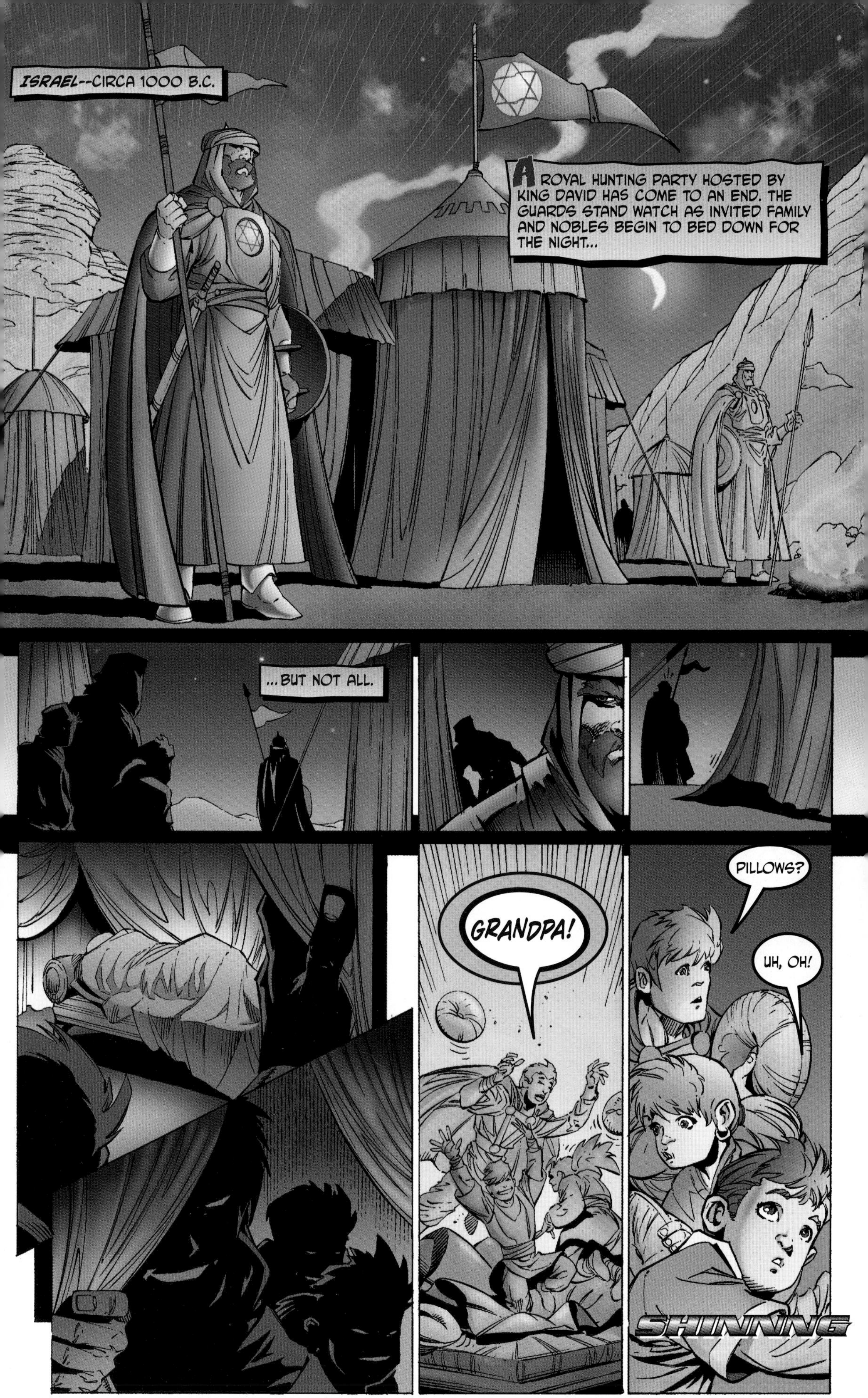
ISRAEL--CIRCA 1000 B.C.
A ROYAL HUNTING PARTY HOSTED BY KING DAVID HAS COME TO AN END. THE GUARDS STAND WATCH AS INVITED FAMILY AND NOBLES BEGIN TO BED DOWN FOR THE NIGHT...
...BUT NOT ALL.
GRANDPA!
PILLOWS?
UH, OH!
SHINNNG

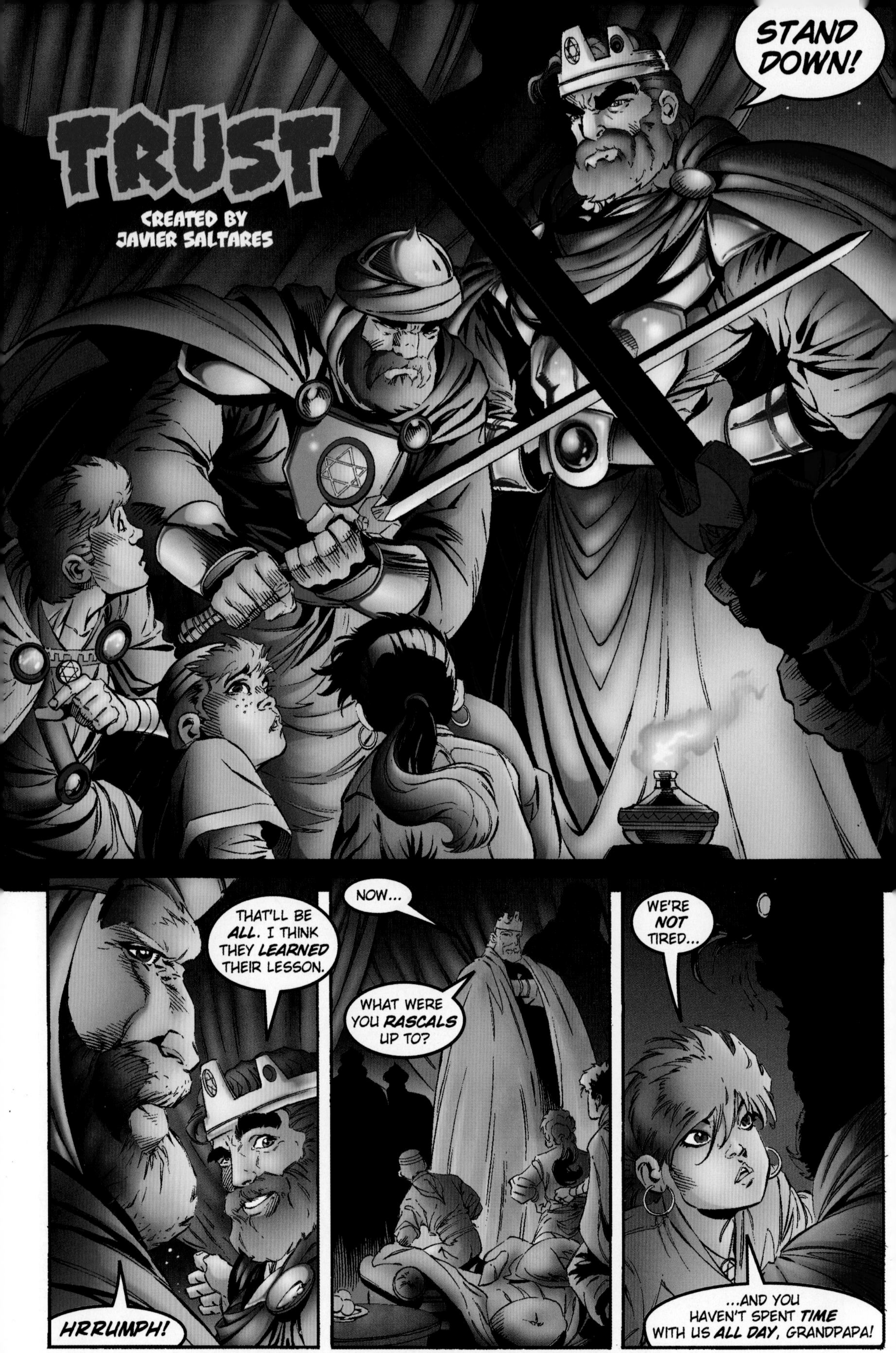
STAND DOWN!
TRUST
CREATED BY JAVIER SALTARES
THAT'LL BE ALL. I THINK THEY LEARNED THEIR LESSON.
HRRUMPH!
NOW...
WHAT WERE YOU RASCALS UP TO?
WE'RE NOT TIRED...
...AND YOU HAVEN'T SPENT TIME WITH US ALL DAY, GRANDPAPA!

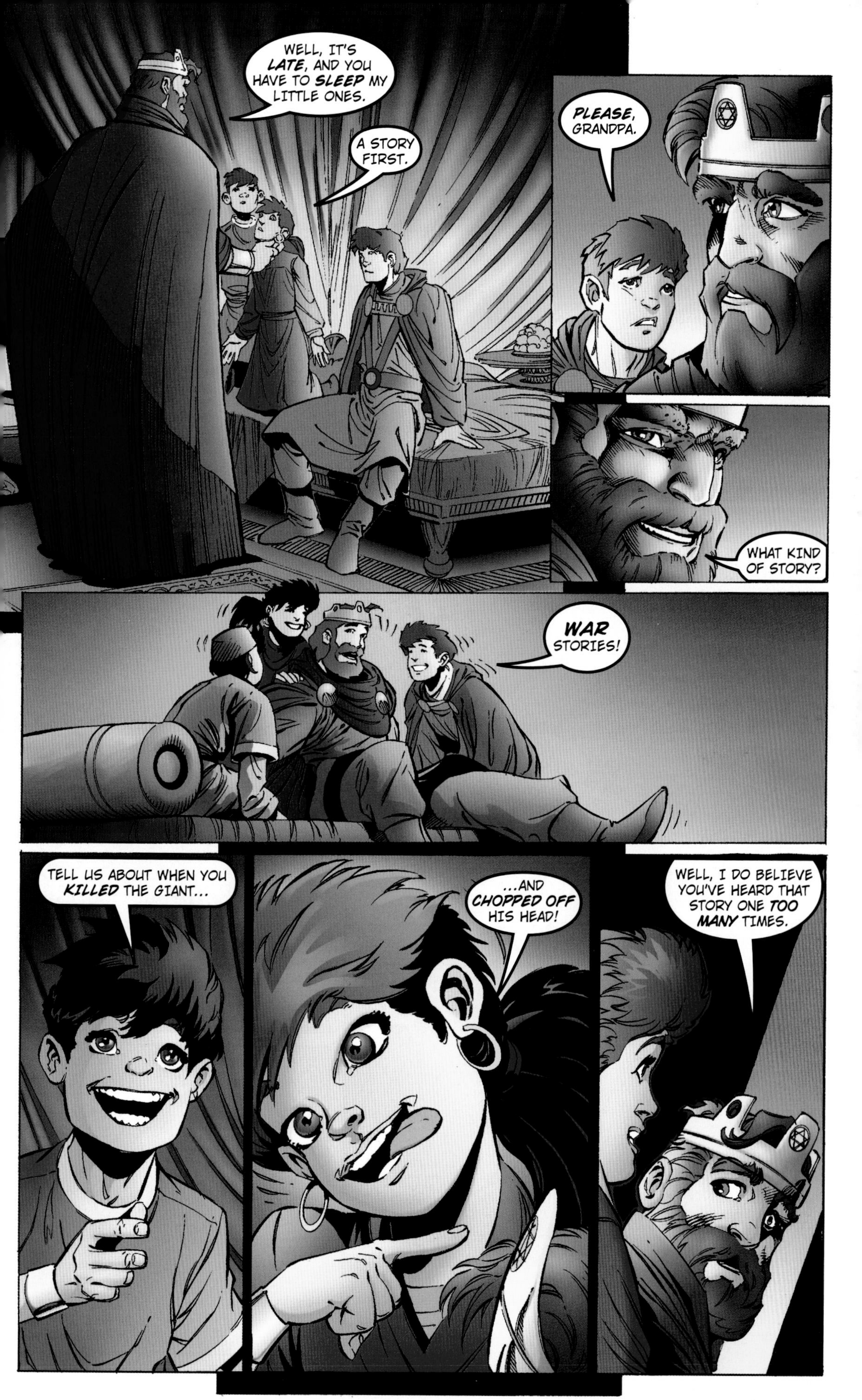
WELL, IT'S *LATE*, AND YOU HAVE TO *SLEEP* MY LITTLE ONES.
A STORY FIRST.
PLEASE, GRANDPA.
WHAT KIND OF STORY?
WAR STORIES!
TELL US ABOUT WHEN YOU *KILLED* THE GIANT...
...AND *CHOPPED OFF* HIS HEAD!
WELL, I DO BELIEVE YOU'VE HEARD THAT STORY ONE *TOO MANY* TIMES.

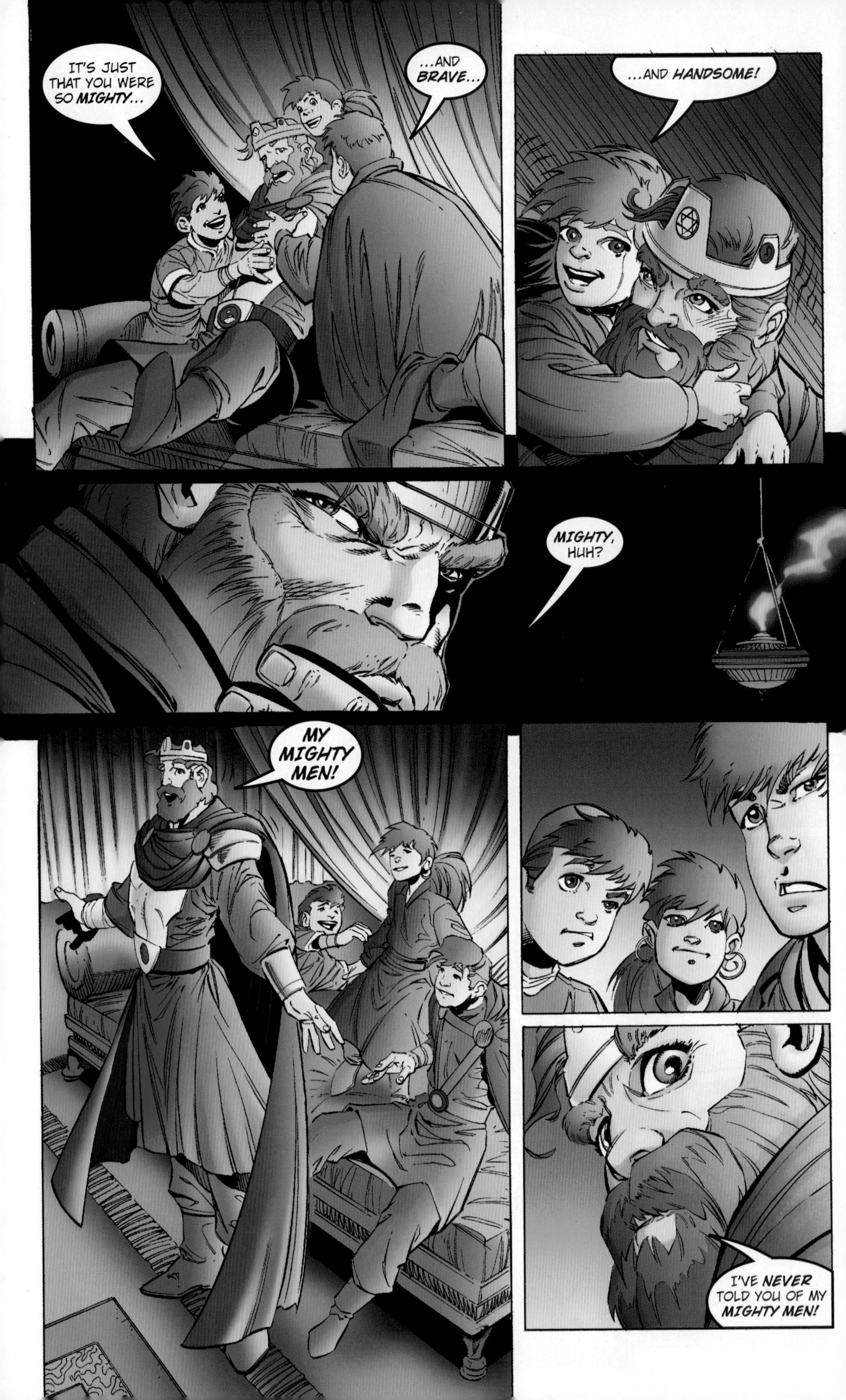
IT'S JUST THAT YOU WERE SO MIGHTY...
...AND BRAVE...
...AND HANDSOME!
MIGHTY, HUH?
MY MIGHTY MEN!
I'VE NEVER TOLD YOU OF MY MIGHTY MEN!

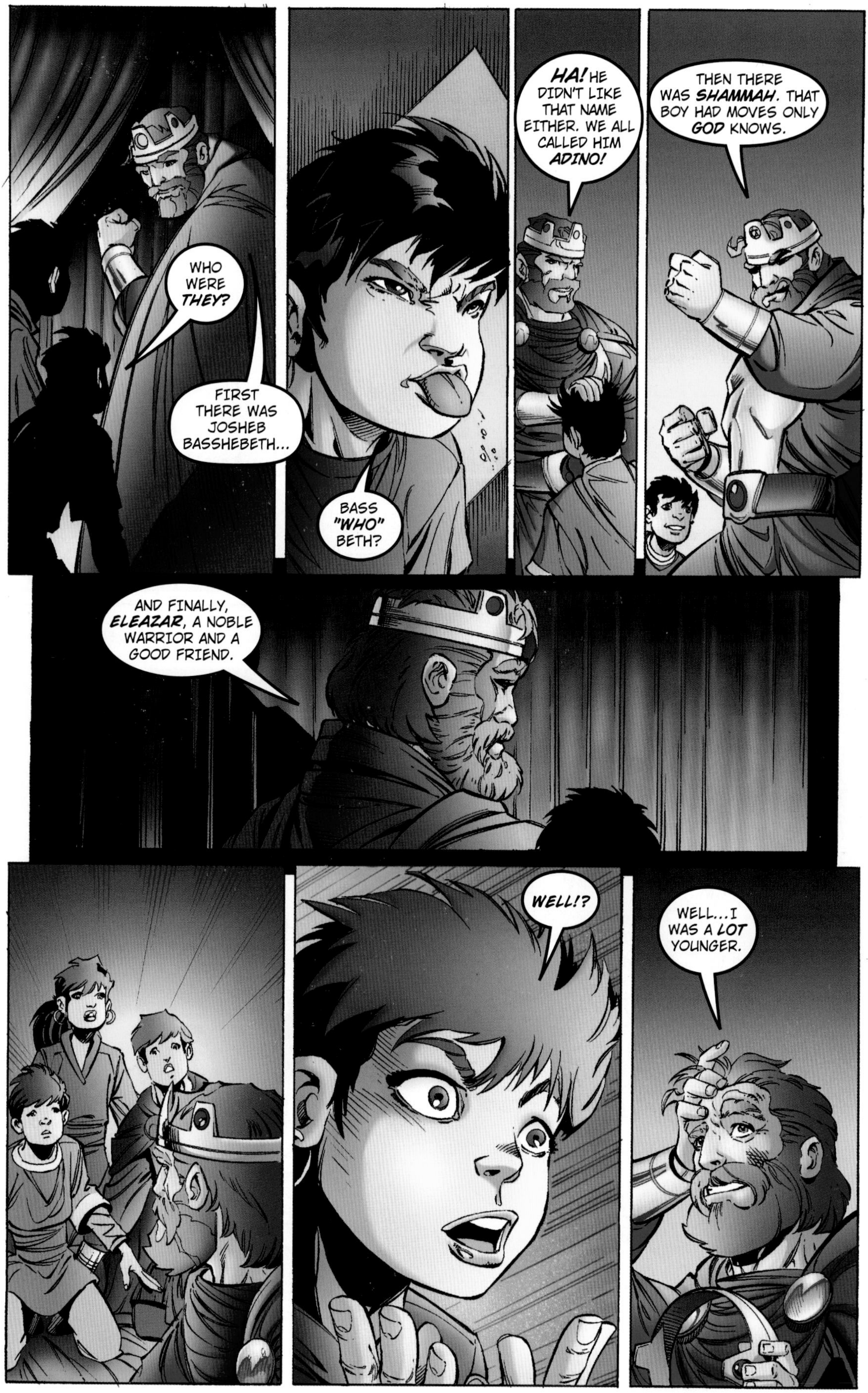
WHO WERE THEY?
FIRST THERE WAS JOSHEB BASSHEBETH...
BASS "WHO" BETH?
HA! HE DIDN'T LIKE THAT NAME EITHER. WE ALL CALLED HIM ADINO!
THEN THERE WAS SHAMMAH. THAT BOY HAD MOVES ONLY GOD KNOWS.
AND FINALLY, ELEAZAR, A NOBLE WARRIOR AND A GOOD FRIEND.
WELL!?
WELL...I WAS A LOT YOUNGER.

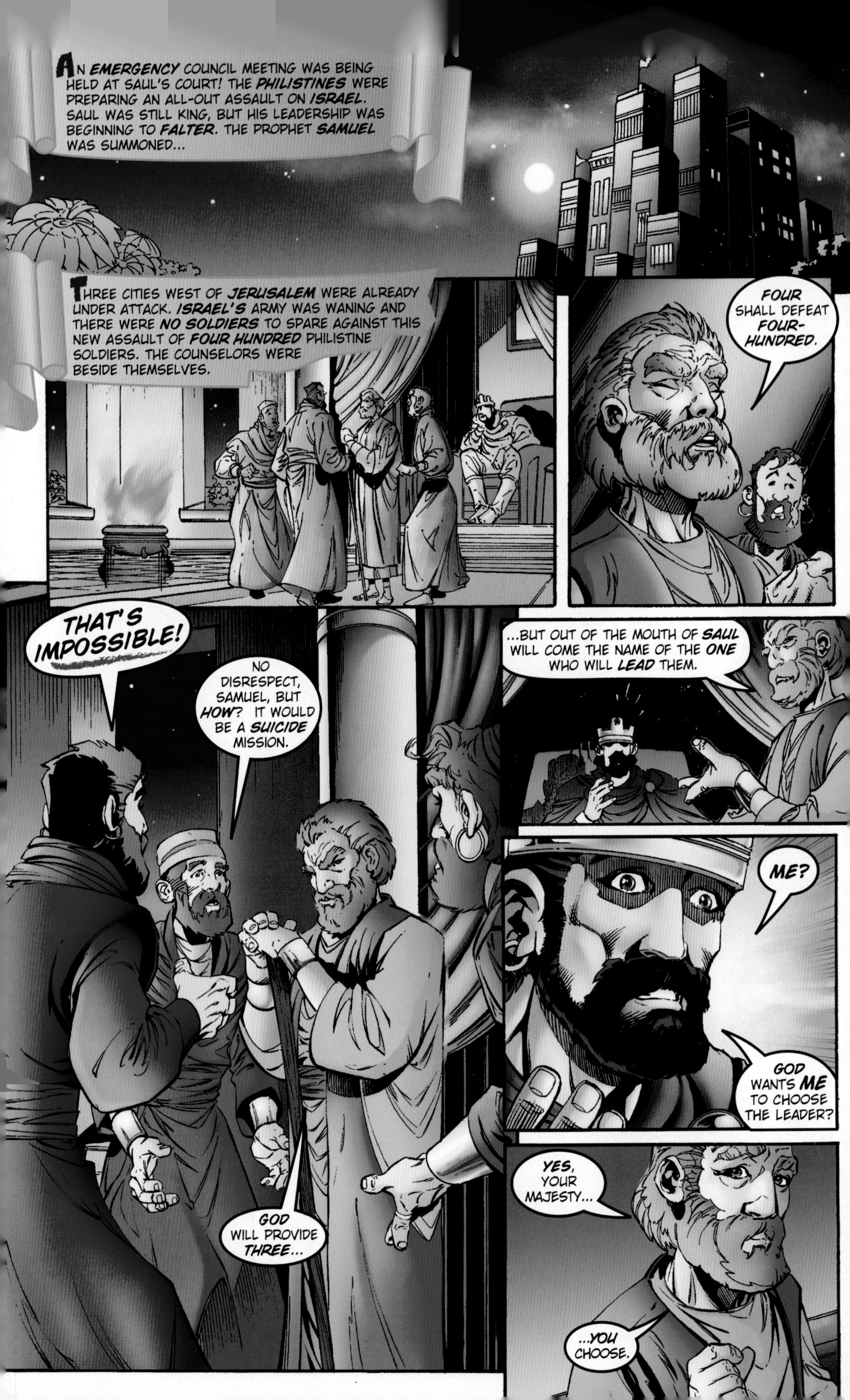
AN EMERGENCY COUNCIL MEETING WAS BEING HELD AT SAUL'S COURT! THE PHILISTINES WERE PREPARING AN ALL-OUT ASSAULT ON ISRAEL. SAUL WAS STILL KING, BUT HIS LEADERSHIP WAS BEGINNING TO FALTER. THE PROPHET SAMUEL WAS SUMMONED...
THREE CITIES WEST OF JERUSALEM WERE ALREADY UNDER ATTACK. ISRAEL'S ARMY WAS WANING AND THERE WERE NO SOLDIERS TO SPARE AGAINST THIS NEW ASSAULT OF FOUR HUNDRED PHILISTINE SOLDIERS. THE COUNSELORS WERE BESIDE THEMSELVES.
FOUR SHALL DEFEAT FOUR-HUNDRED.
THAT'S IMPOSSIBLE!
NO DISRESPECT, SAMUEL, BUT HOW? IT WOULD BE A SUICIDE MISSION.
GOD WILL PROVIDE THREE...
...BUT OUT OF THE MOUTH OF SAUL WILL COME THE NAME OF THE ONE WHO WILL LEAD THEM.
ME?
GOD WANTS ME TO CHOOSE THE LEADER?
YES, YOUR MAJESTY...
...YOU CHOOSE.

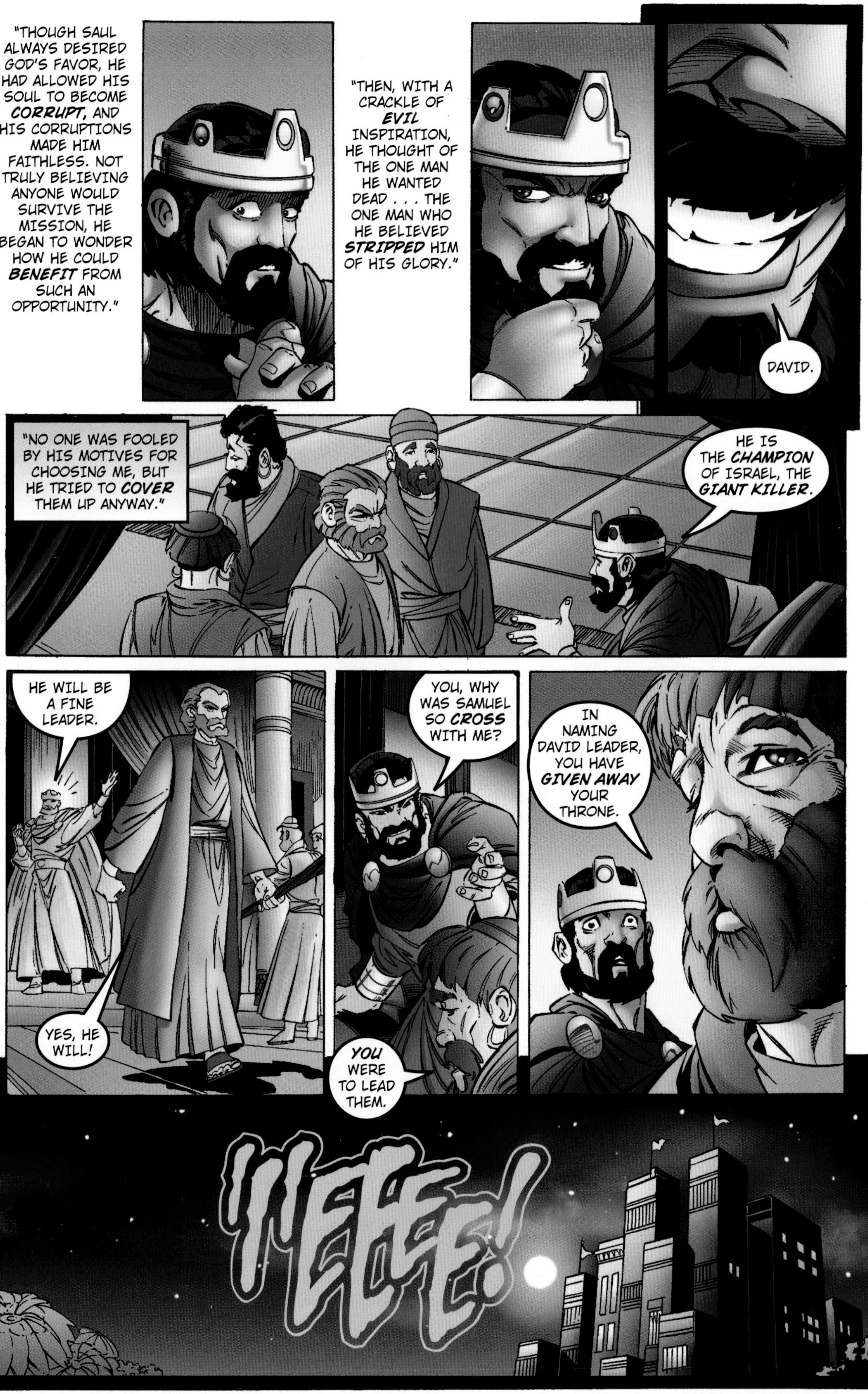
"THOUGH SAUL ALWAYS DESIRED GOD'S FAVOR, HE HAD ALLOWED HIS SOUL TO BECOME CORRUPT, AND HIS CORRUPTIONS MADE HIM FAITHLESS. NOT TRULY BELIEVING ANYONE WOULD SURVIVE THE MISSION, HE BEGAN TO WONDER HOW HE COULD BENEFIT FROM SUCH AN OPPORTUNITY."
"THEN, WITH A CRACKLE OF EVIL INSPIRATION, HE THOUGHT OF THE ONE MAN HE WANTED DEAD . . . THE ONE MAN WHO HE BELIEVED STRIPPED HIM OF HIS GLORY."
DAVID.
"NO ONE WAS FOOLED BY HIS MOTIVES FOR CHOOSING ME, BUT HE TRIED TO COVER THEM UP ANYWAY."
HE IS THE CHAMPION OF ISRAEL, THE GIANT KILLER.
HE WILL BE A FINE LEADER.
YES, HE WILL!
YOU, WHY WAS SAMUEL SO CROSS WITH ME?
YOU WERE TO LEAD THEM.
IN NAMING DAVID LEADER, YOU HAVE GIVEN AWAY YOUR THRONE.

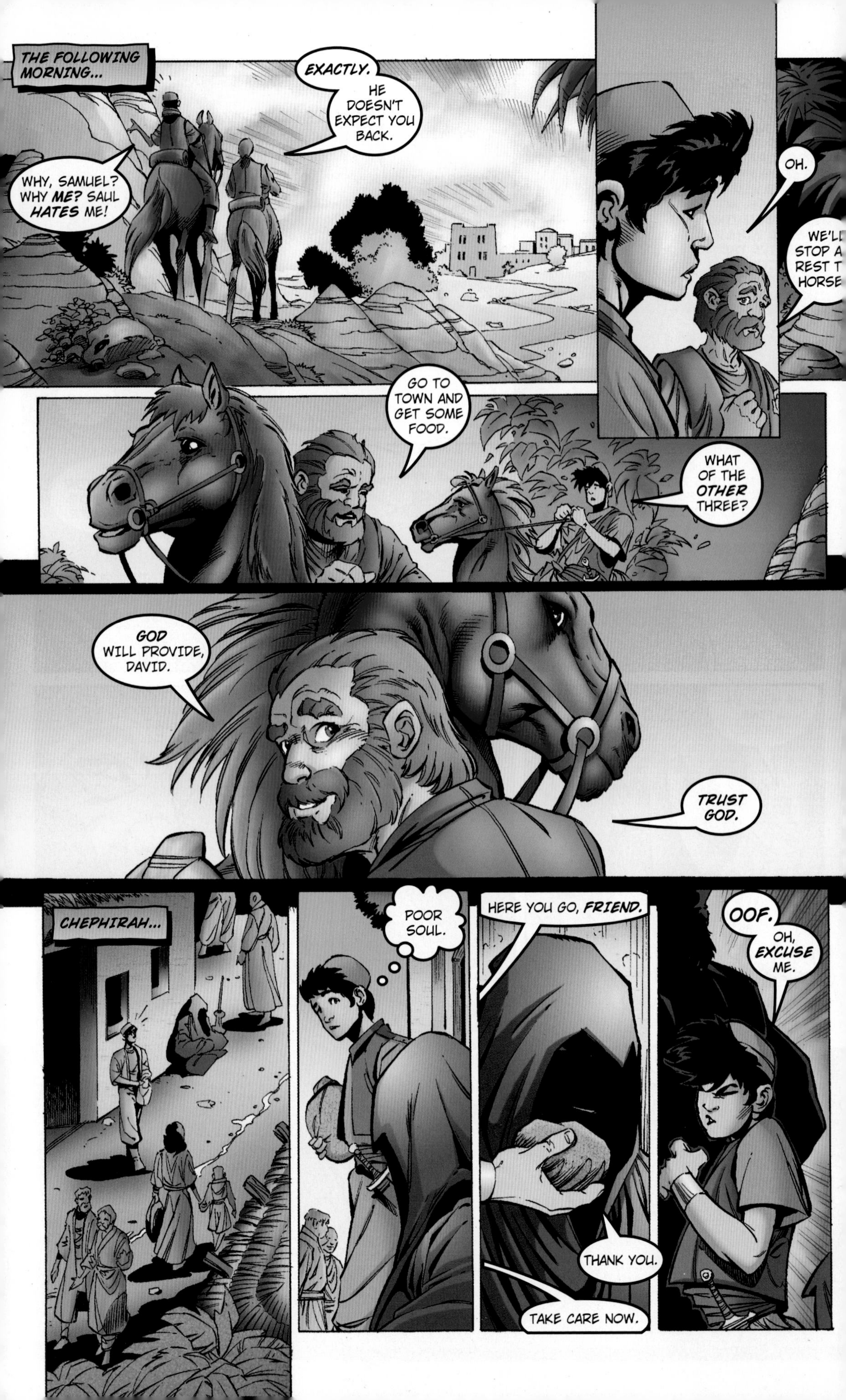
THE FOLLOWING MORNING...
WHY, SAMUEL? WHY ME? SAUL HATES ME!
EXACTLY. HE DOESN'T EXPECT YOU BACK.
OH.
WE'LL STOP A REST T HORSE
GO TO TOWN AND GET SOME FOOD.
WHAT OF THE OTHER THREE?
GOD WILL PROVIDE, DAVID.
TRUST GOD.
CHEPHIRAH...
POOR SOUL.
HERE YOU GO, FRIEND.
THANK YOU.
TAKE CARE NOW.
OOF.
OH, EXCUSE ME.

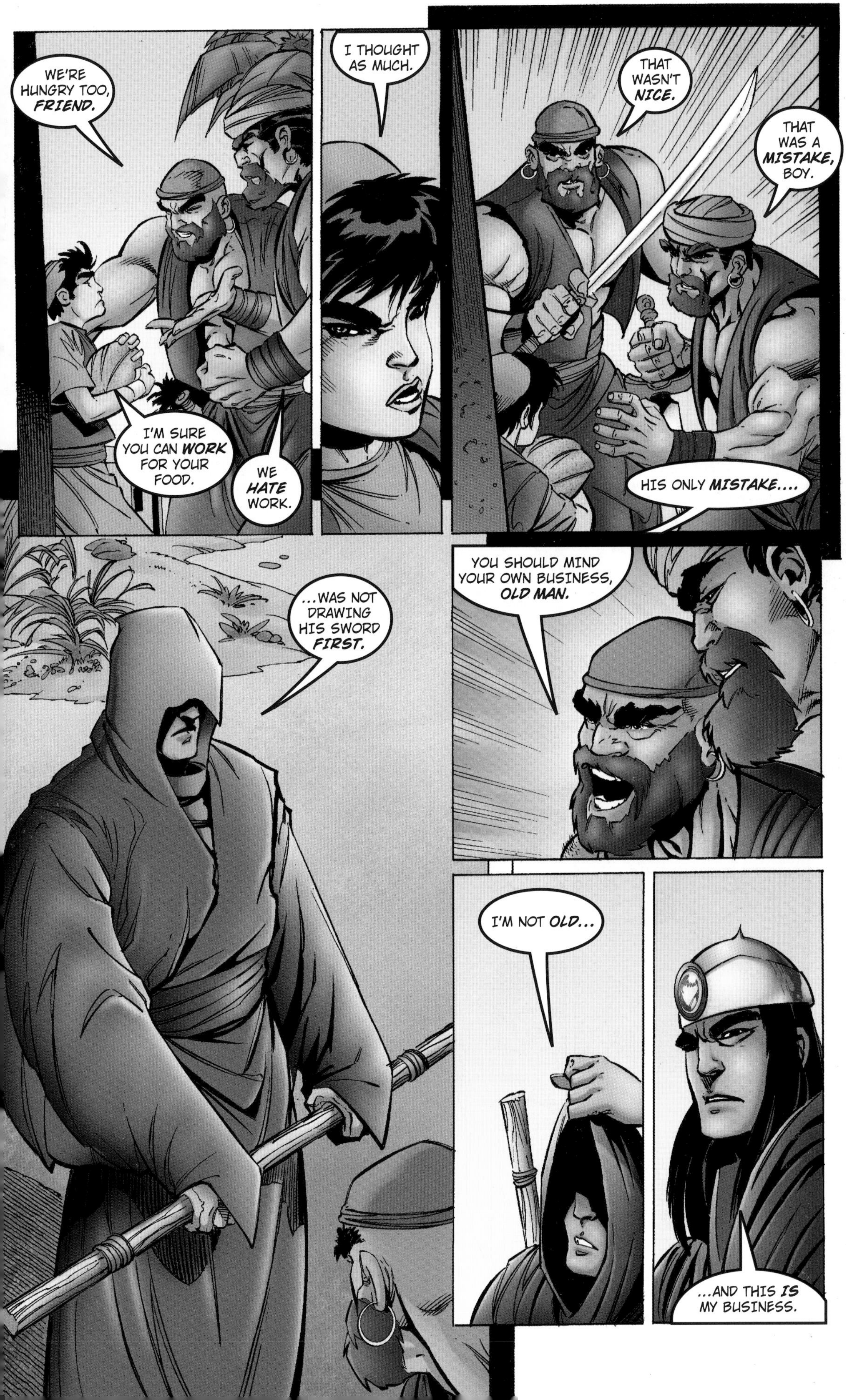
WE'RE HUNGRY TOO, FRIEND.
I'M SURE YOU CAN WORK FOR YOUR FOOD.
WE HATE WORK.
I THOUGHT AS MUCH.
THAT WASN'T NICE.
THAT WAS A MISTAKE, BOY.
HIS ONLY MISTAKE....
...WAS NOT DRAWING HIS SWORD FIRST.
YOU SHOULD MIND YOUR OWN BUSINESS, OLD MAN.
I'M NOT OLD...
...AND THIS IS MY BUSINESS.

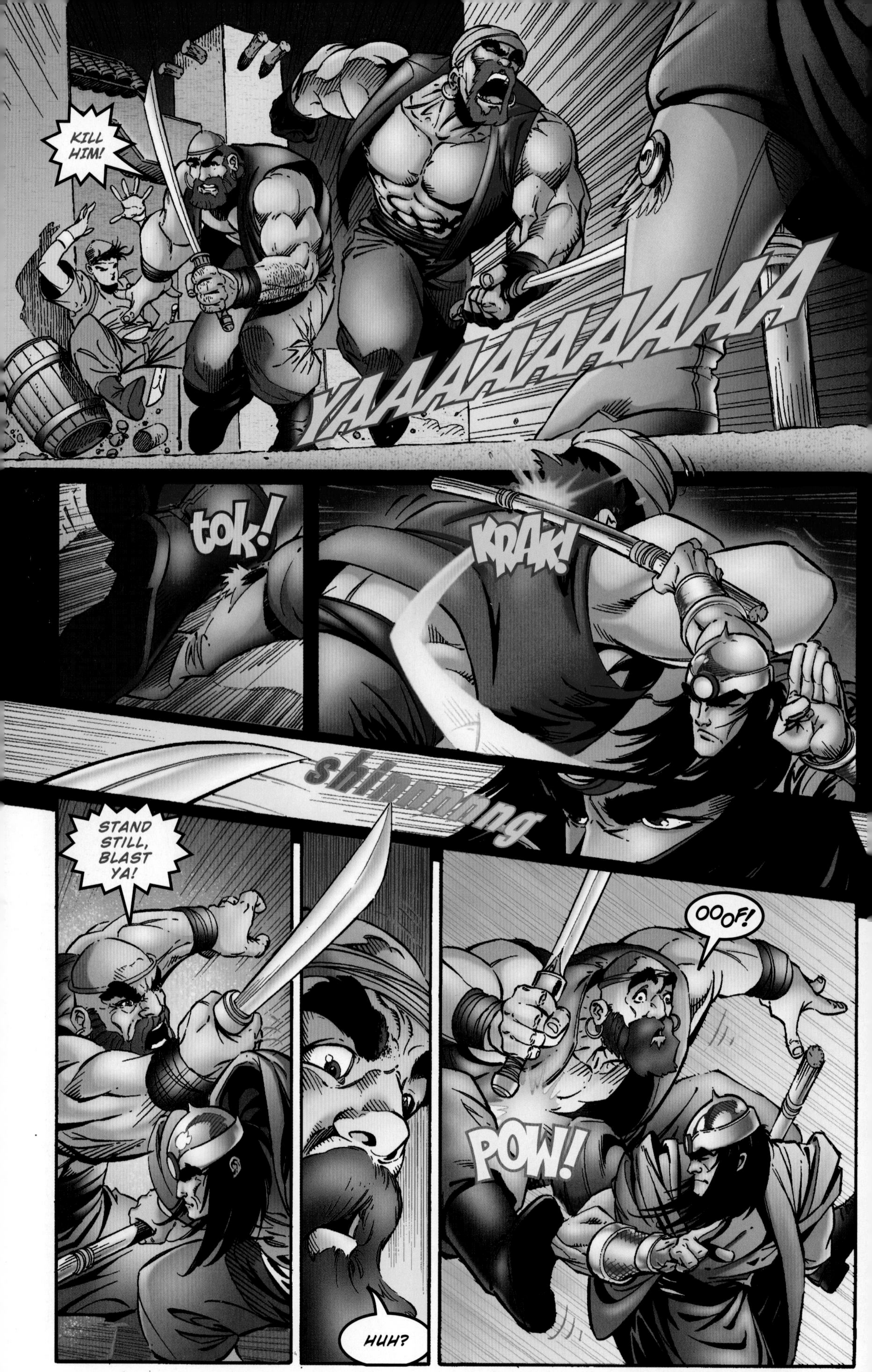
KILL HIM!
YAAAAAAAAAAA
tok!
KRAK!
shinnnnng
STAND STILL, BLAST YA!
HUH?
OOOF!
POW!

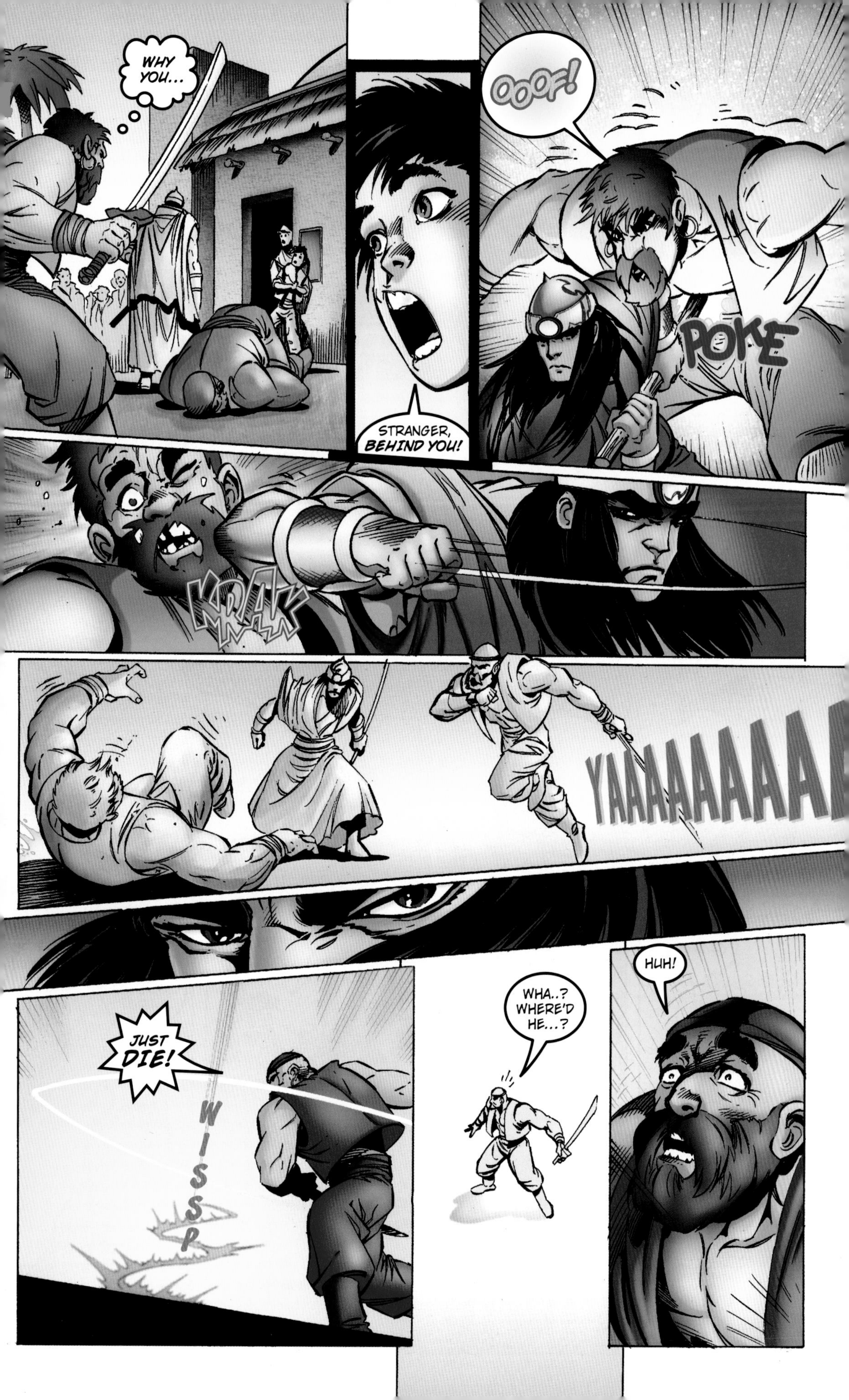
WHY YOU...
STRANGER, BEHIND YOU!
OOOF!
POKE
KRAK
YAAAAAAAA
JUST DIE!
WISSP
WHA..? WHERE'D HE...?
HUH!

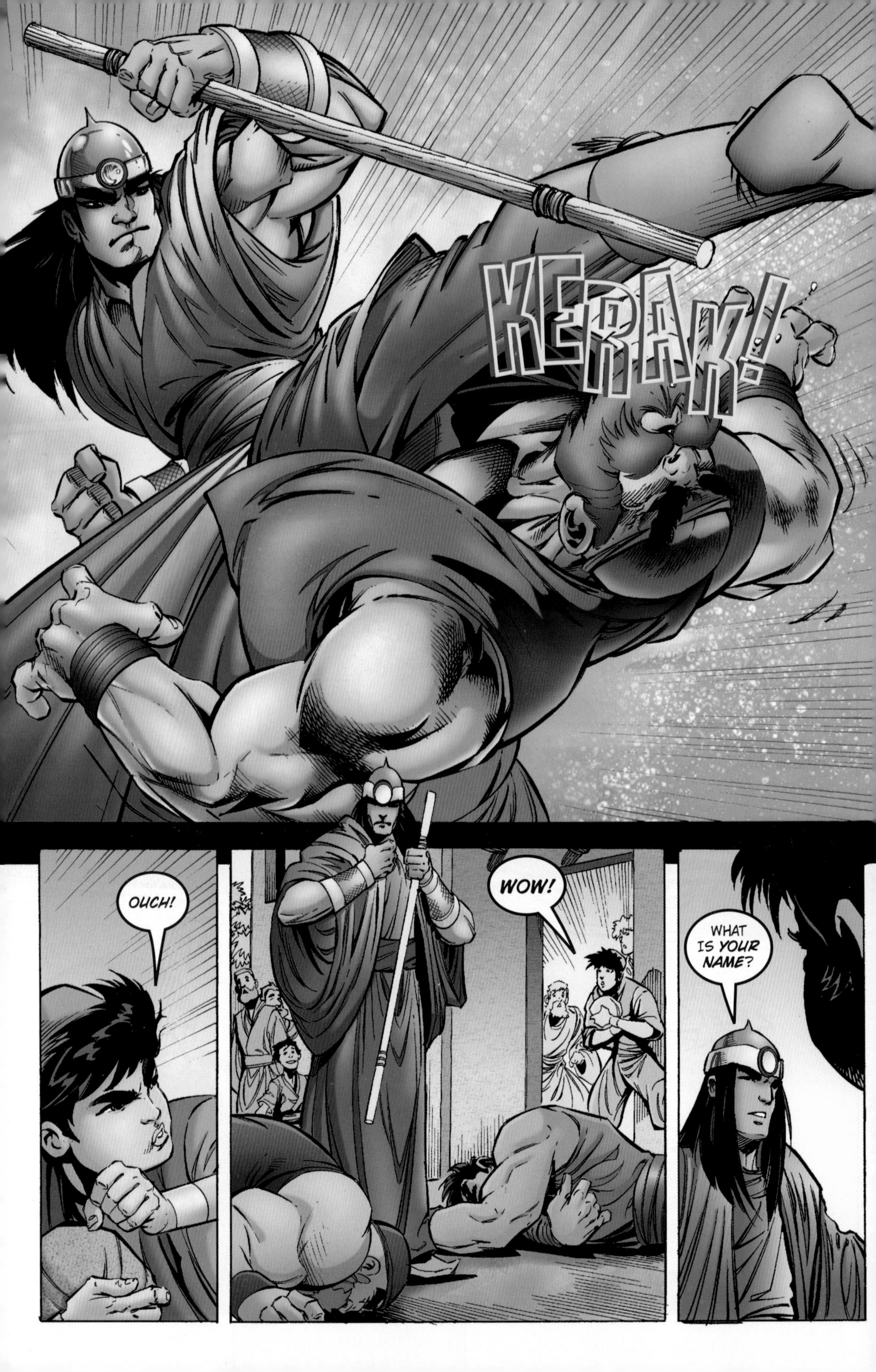
KERAK!
OUCH!
WOW!
WHAT IS YOUR NAME?

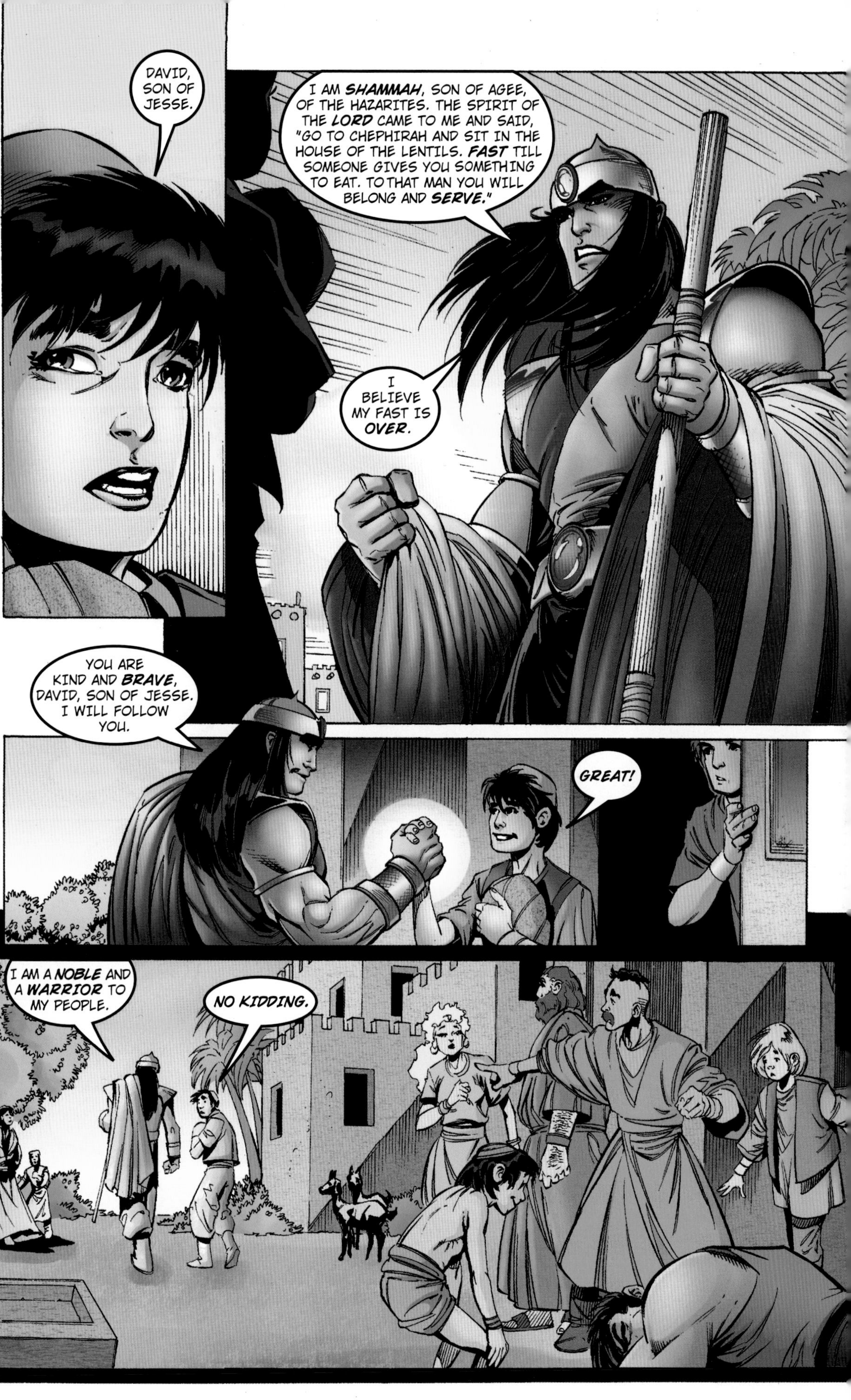
DAVID, SON OF JESSE.
I AM SHAMMAH, SON OF AGEE, OF THE HAZARITES. THE SPIRIT OF THE LORD CAME TO ME AND SAID, "GO TO CHEPHIRAH AND SIT IN THE HOUSE OF THE LENTILS. FAST TILL SOMEONE GIVES YOU SOMETHING TO EAT. TO THAT MAN YOU WILL BELONG AND SERVE."
I BELIEVE MY FAST IS OVER.
YOU ARE KIND AND BRAVE, DAVID, SON OF JESSE. I WILL FOLLOW YOU.
GREAT!
I AM A NOBLE AND A WARRIOR TO MY PEOPLE.
NO KIDDING.

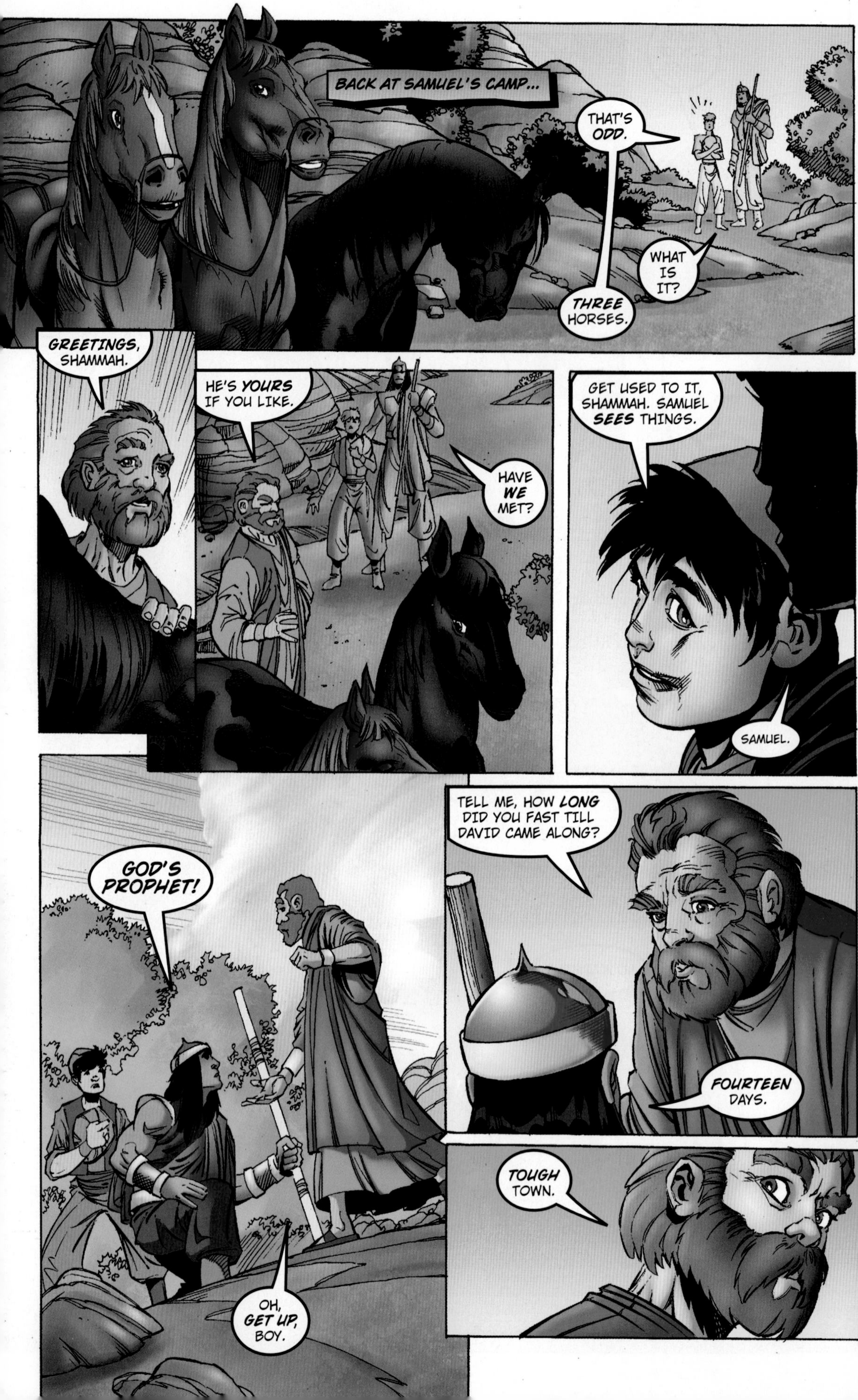
BACK AT SAMUEL'S CAMP...
THAT'S ODD.
WHAT IS IT?
THREE HORSES.
GREETINGS, SHAMMAH.
HE'S YOURS IF YOU LIKE.
HAVE WE MET?
GET USED TO IT, SHAMMAH. SAMUEL SEES THINGS.
SAMUEL.
GOD'S PROPHET!
OH, GET UP, BOY.
TELL ME, HOW LONG DID YOU FAST TILL DAVID CAME ALONG?
FOURTEEN DAYS.
TOUGH TOWN.

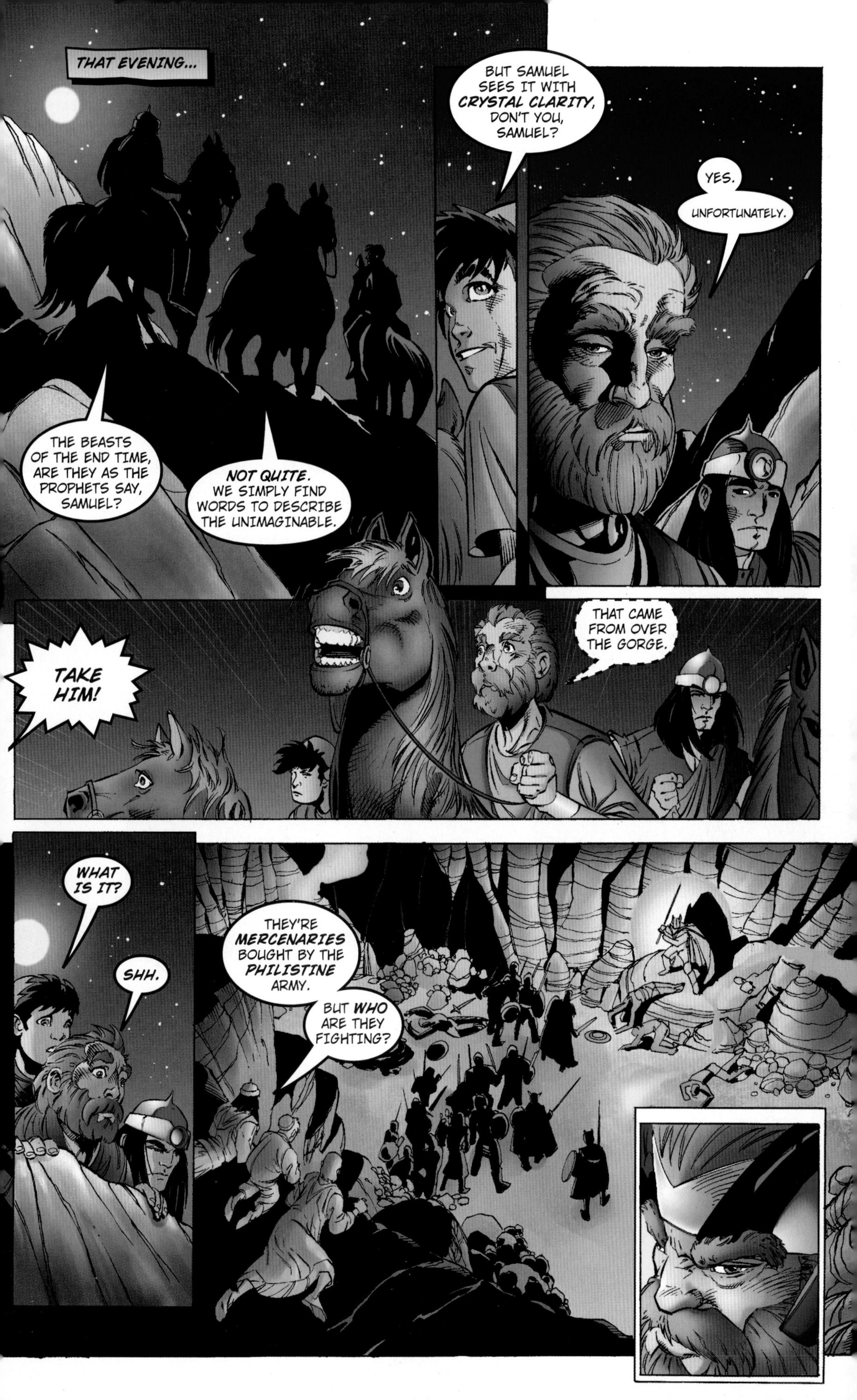
THAT EVENING...
BUT SAMUEL SEES IT WITH CRYSTAL CLARITY, DON'T YOU, SAMUEL?
YES.
UNFORTUNATELY.
THE BEASTS OF THE END TIME, ARE THEY AS THE PROPHETS SAY, SAMUEL?
NOT QUITE. WE SIMPLY FIND WORDS TO DESCRIBE THE UNIMAGINABLE.
TAKE HIM!
THAT CAME FROM OVER THE GORGE.
WHAT IS IT?
SHH.
THEY'RE MERCENARIES BOUGHT BY THE PHILISTINE ARMY.
BUT WHO ARE THEY FIGHTING?

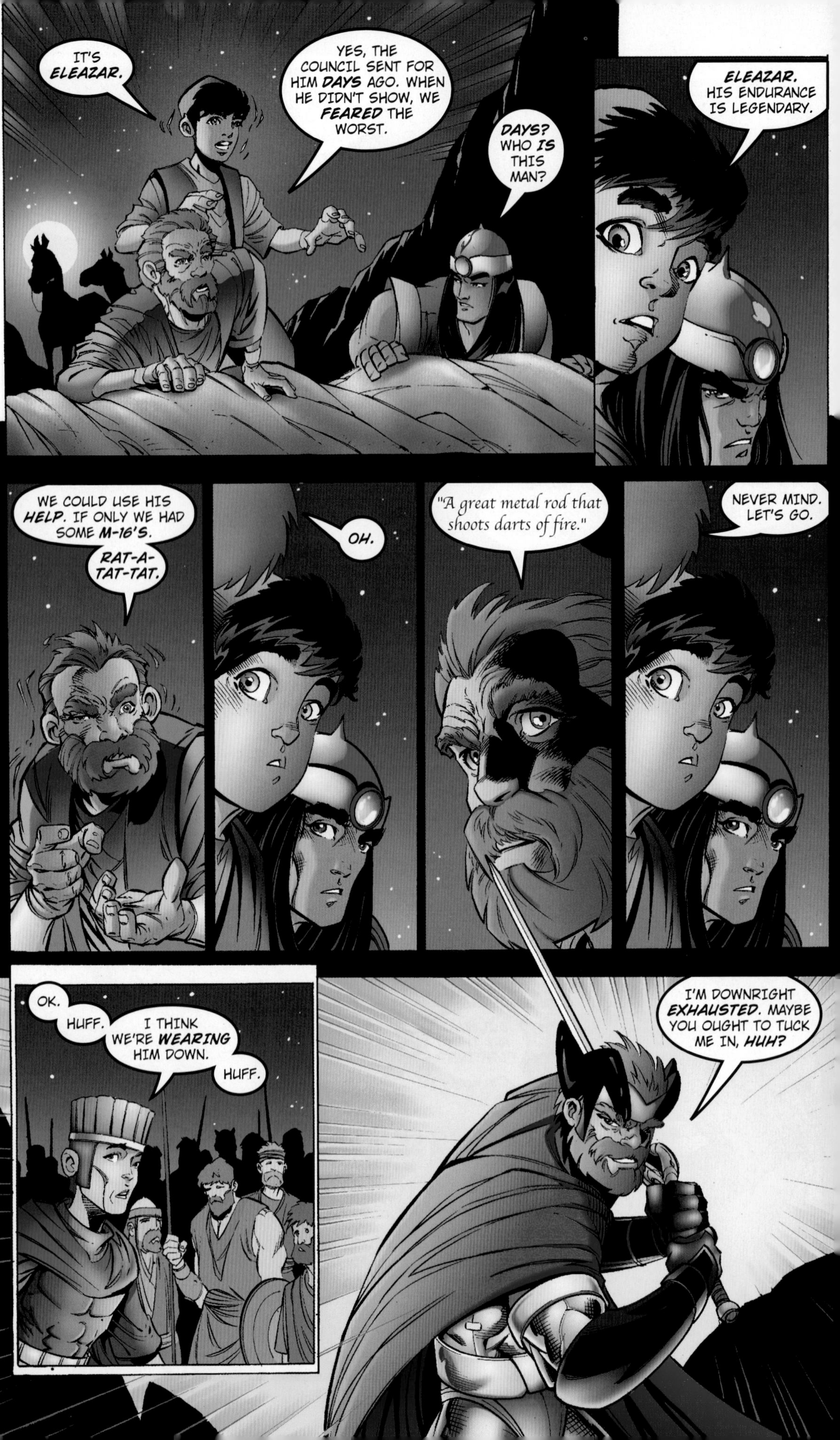
IT'S *ELEAZAR.*
YES, THE COUNCIL SENT FOR HIM *DAYS* AGO. WHEN HE DIDN'T SHOW, WE *FEARED* THE WORST.
DAYS? WHO *IS* THIS MAN?
ELEAZAR. HIS ENDURANCE IS LEGENDARY.
WE COULD USE HIS *HELP*. IF ONLY WE HAD SOME *M-16'S*.
RAT-A-TAT-TAT.
OH.
"A great metal rod that shoots darts of fire."
NEVER MIND. LET'S GO.
OK.
HUFF.
I THINK WE'RE *WEARING* HIM DOWN.
HUFF.
I'M DOWNRIGHT *EXHAUSTED*. MAYBE YOU OUGHT TO TUCK ME IN, *HUH?*

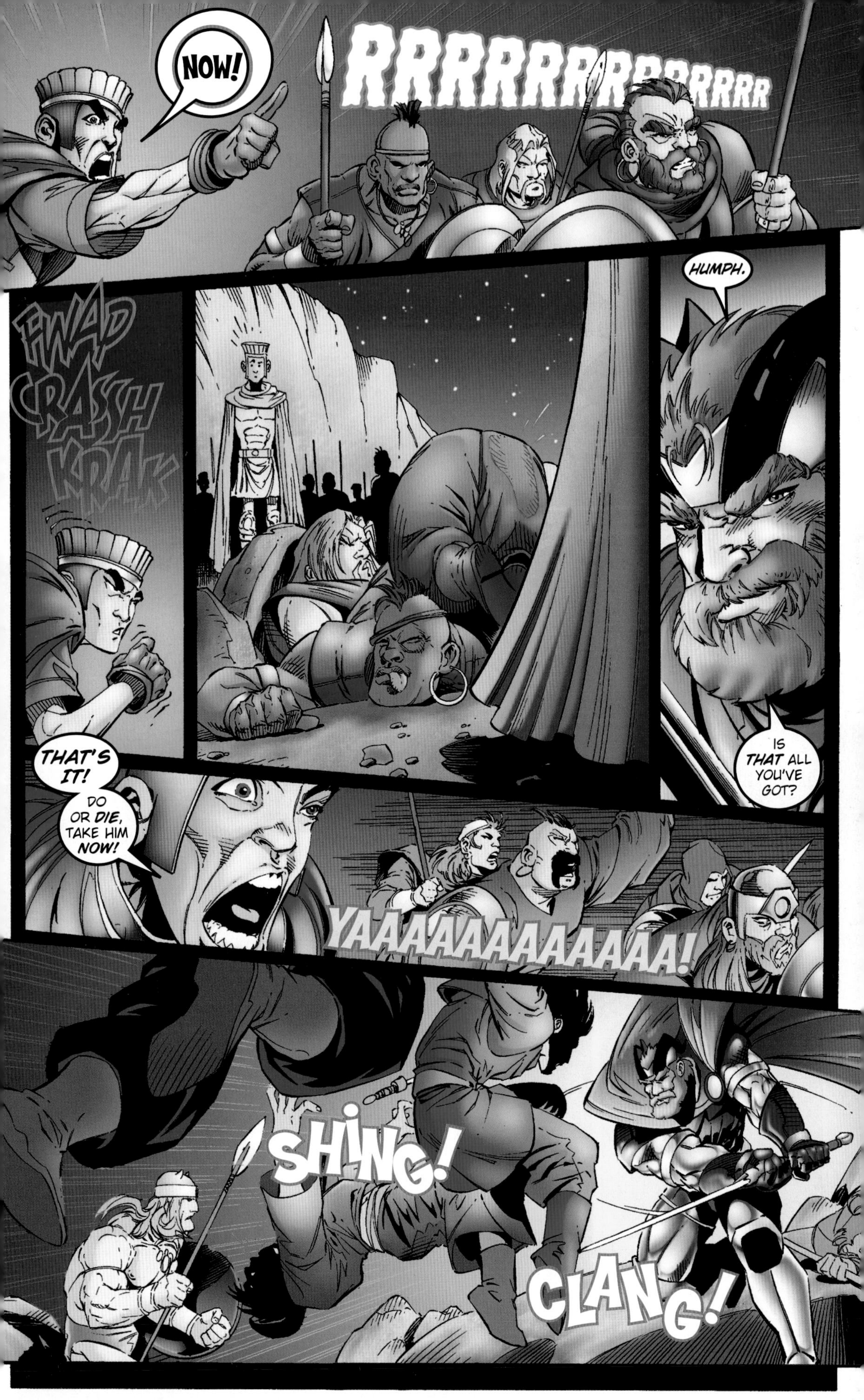
NOW!
RRRRRRRRRRRRRR
FWAP
CRASH
KRAK
HUMPH.
IS THAT ALL YOU'VE GOT?
THAT'S IT!
DO OR DIE, TAKE HIM NOW!
YAAAAAAAAAAAAA!
SHING!
CLANG!

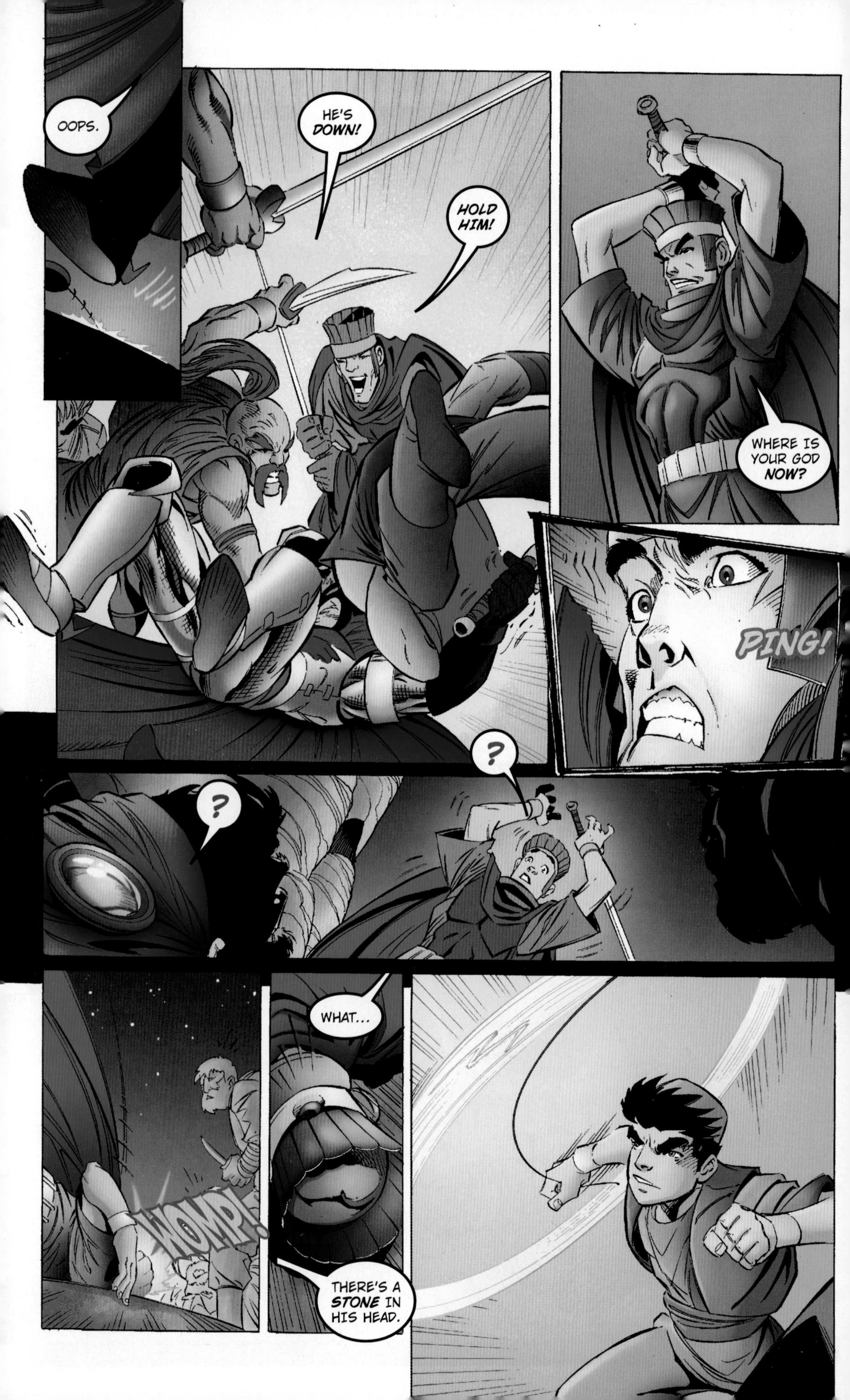
OOPS.
HE'S DOWN!
HOLD HIM!
WHERE IS YOUR GOD NOW?
PING!
?
?
WHAT...
WOMP!
THERE'S A STONE IN HIS HEAD.

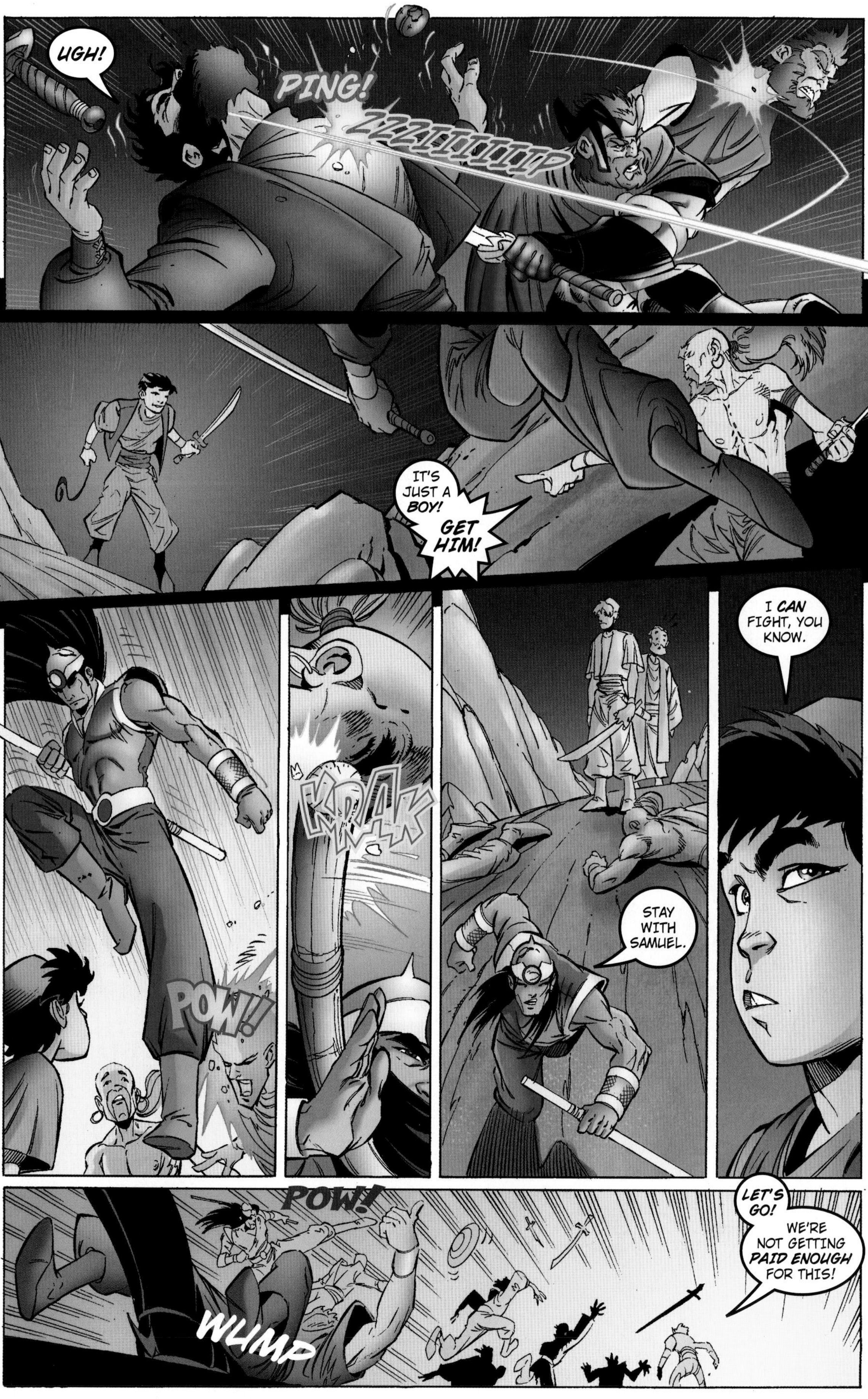
UGH!
PING!
ZZZIIIIIIIIP
IT'S JUST A BOY! GET HIM!
POW!!
KRAK
STAY WITH SAMUEL.
I CAN FIGHT, YOU KNOW.
POW!
WUMP
LET'S GO!
WE'RE NOT GETTING PAID ENOUGH FOR THIS!

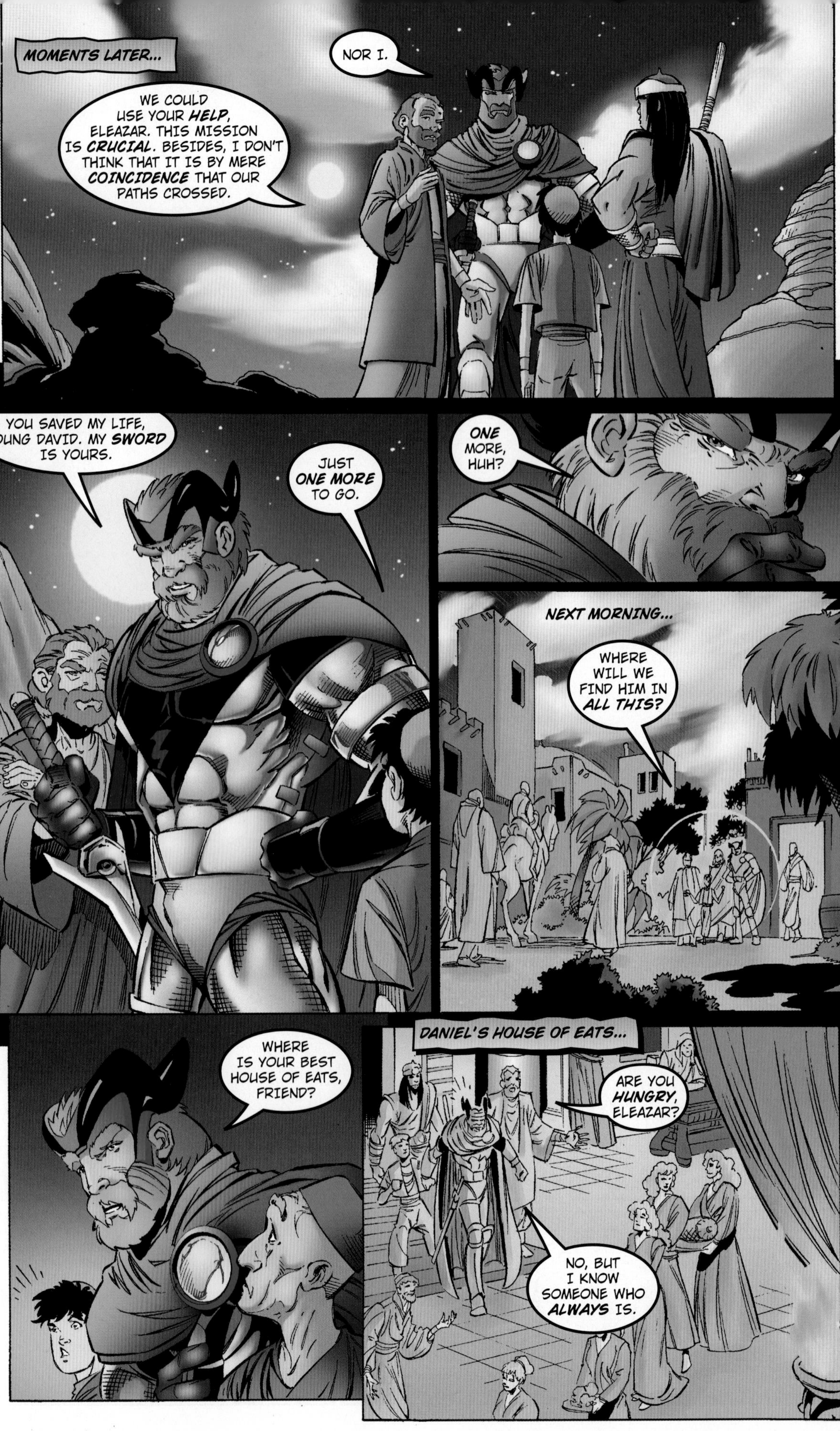
MOMENTS LATER...
NOR I.
WE COULD USE YOUR HELP, ELEAZAR. THIS MISSION IS CRUCIAL. BESIDES, I DON'T THINK THAT IT IS BY MERE COINCIDENCE THAT OUR PATHS CROSSED.
YOU SAVED MY LIFE, YOUNG DAVID. MY SWORD IS YOURS.
JUST ONE MORE TO GO.
ONE MORE, HUH?
NEXT MORNING...
WHERE WILL WE FIND HIM IN ALL THIS?
WHERE IS YOUR BEST HOUSE OF EATS, FRIEND?
DANIEL'S HOUSE OF EATS...
ARE YOU HUNGRY, ELEAZAR?
NO, BUT I KNOW SOMEONE WHO ALWAYS IS.

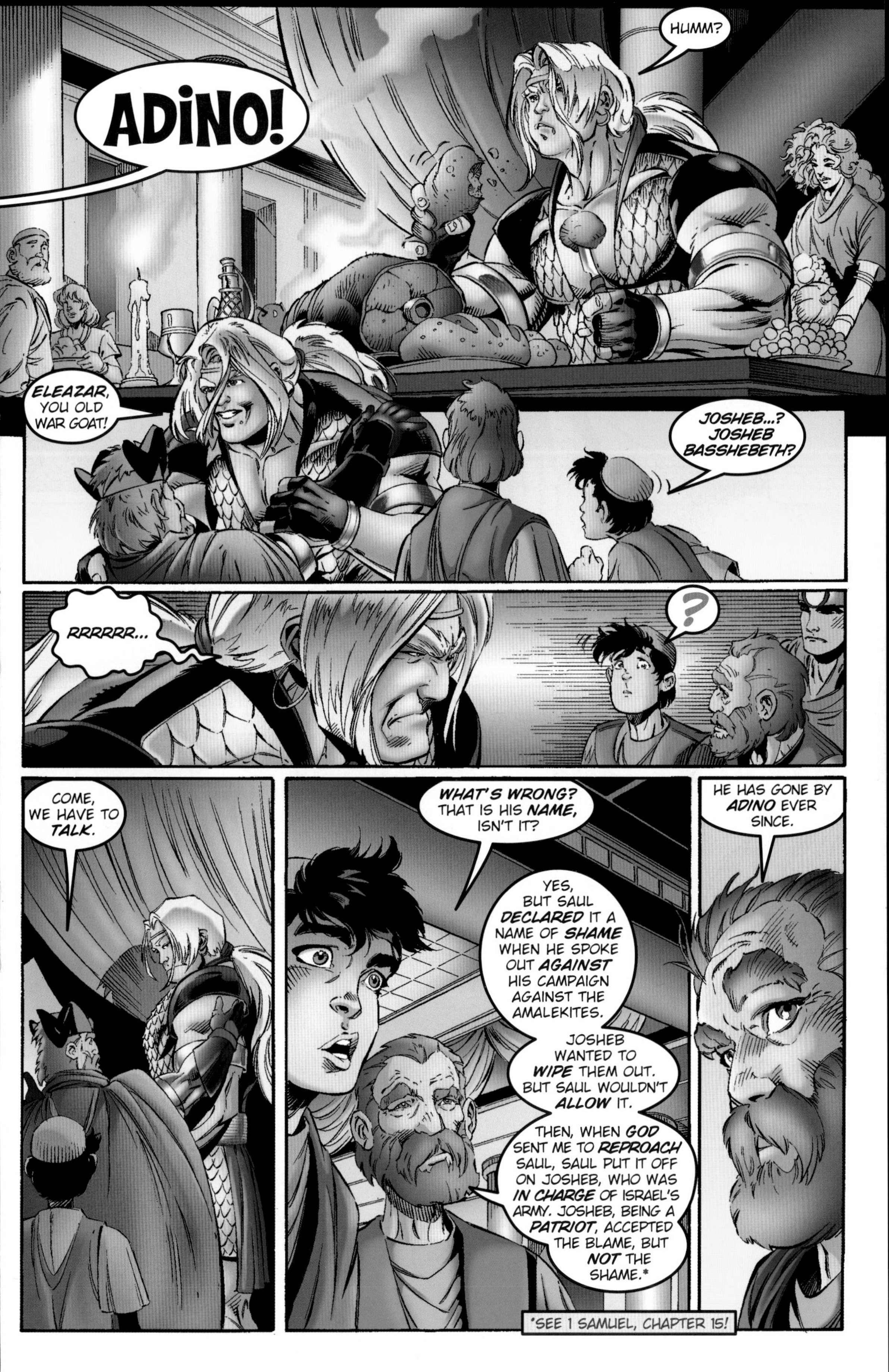
ADINO!
HUMM?
ELEAZAR, YOU OLD WAR GOAT!
JOSHEB...? JOSHEB BASSHEBETH?
RRRRRR...
?
COME, WE HAVE TO TALK.
WHAT'S WRONG? THAT IS HIS NAME, ISN'T IT?
YES, BUT SAUL DECLARED IT A NAME OF SHAME WHEN HE SPOKE OUT AGAINST HIS CAMPAIGN AGAINST THE AMALEKITES.
JOSHEB WANTED TO WIPE THEM OUT. BUT SAUL WOULDN'T ALLOW IT.
THEN, WHEN GOD SENT ME TO REPROACH SAUL, SAUL PUT IT OFF ON JOSHEB, WHO WAS IN CHARGE OF ISRAEL'S ARMY. JOSHEB, BEING A PATRIOT, ACCEPTED THE BLAME, BUT NOT THE SHAME.*
HE HAS GONE BY ADINO EVER SINCE.
*SEE 1 SAMUEL, CHAPTER 15!

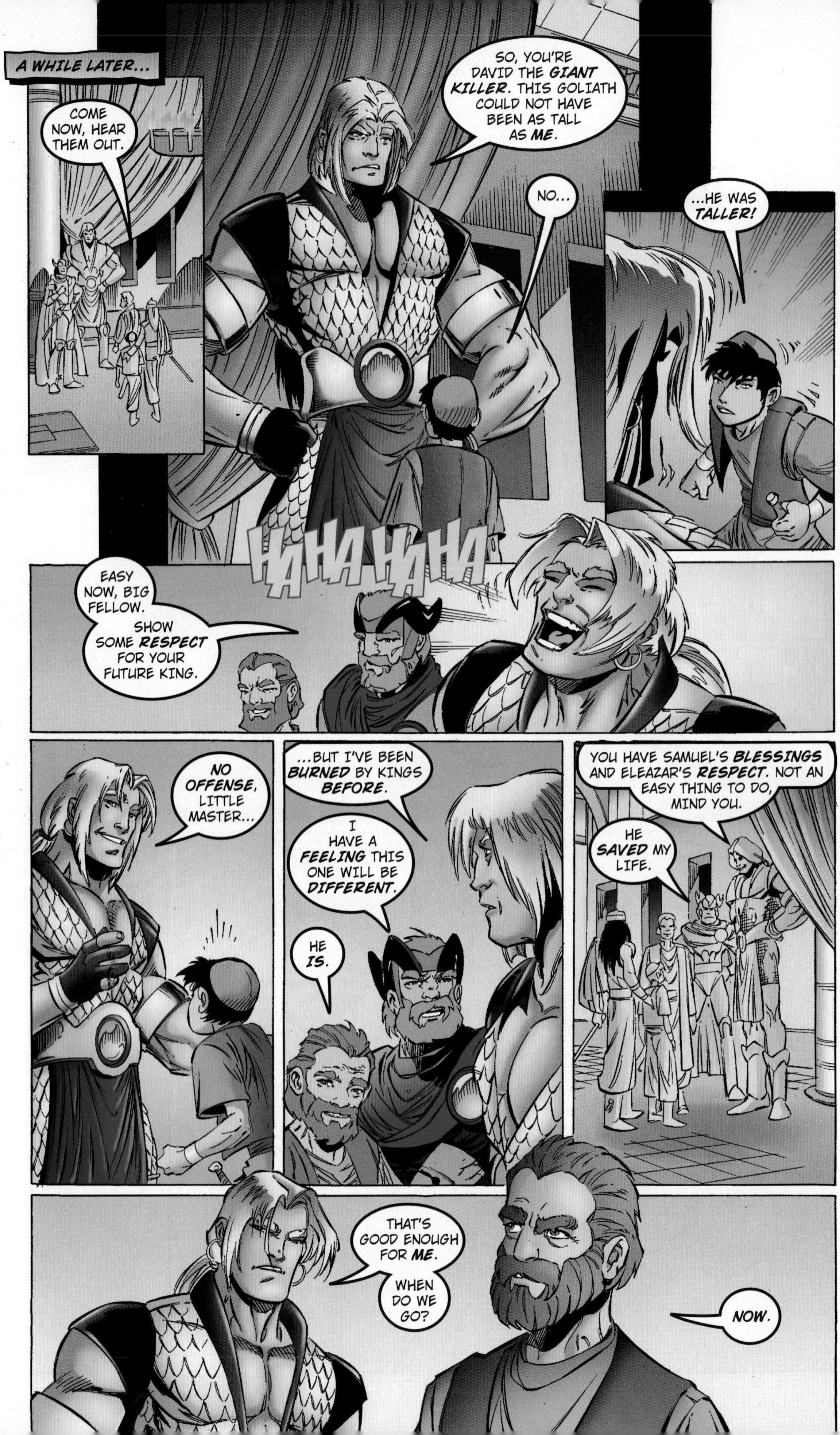
A WHILE LATER...
COME NOW, HEAR THEM OUT.
SO, YOU'RE DAVID THE GIANT KILLER. THIS GOLIATH COULD NOT HAVE BEEN AS TALL AS ME.
NO...
...HE WAS TALLER!
HAHA HAHA
EASY NOW, BIG FELLOW.
SHOW SOME RESPECT FOR YOUR FUTURE KING.
NO OFFENSE, LITTLE MASTER...
...BUT I'VE BEEN BURNED BY KINGS BEFORE.
I HAVE A FEELING THIS ONE WILL BE DIFFERENT.
HE IS.
YOU HAVE SAMUEL'S BLESSINGS AND ELEAZAR'S RESPECT. NOT AN EASY THING TO DO, MIND YOU.
HE SAVED MY LIFE.
THAT'S GOOD ENOUGH FOR ME.
WHEN DO WE GO?
NOW.

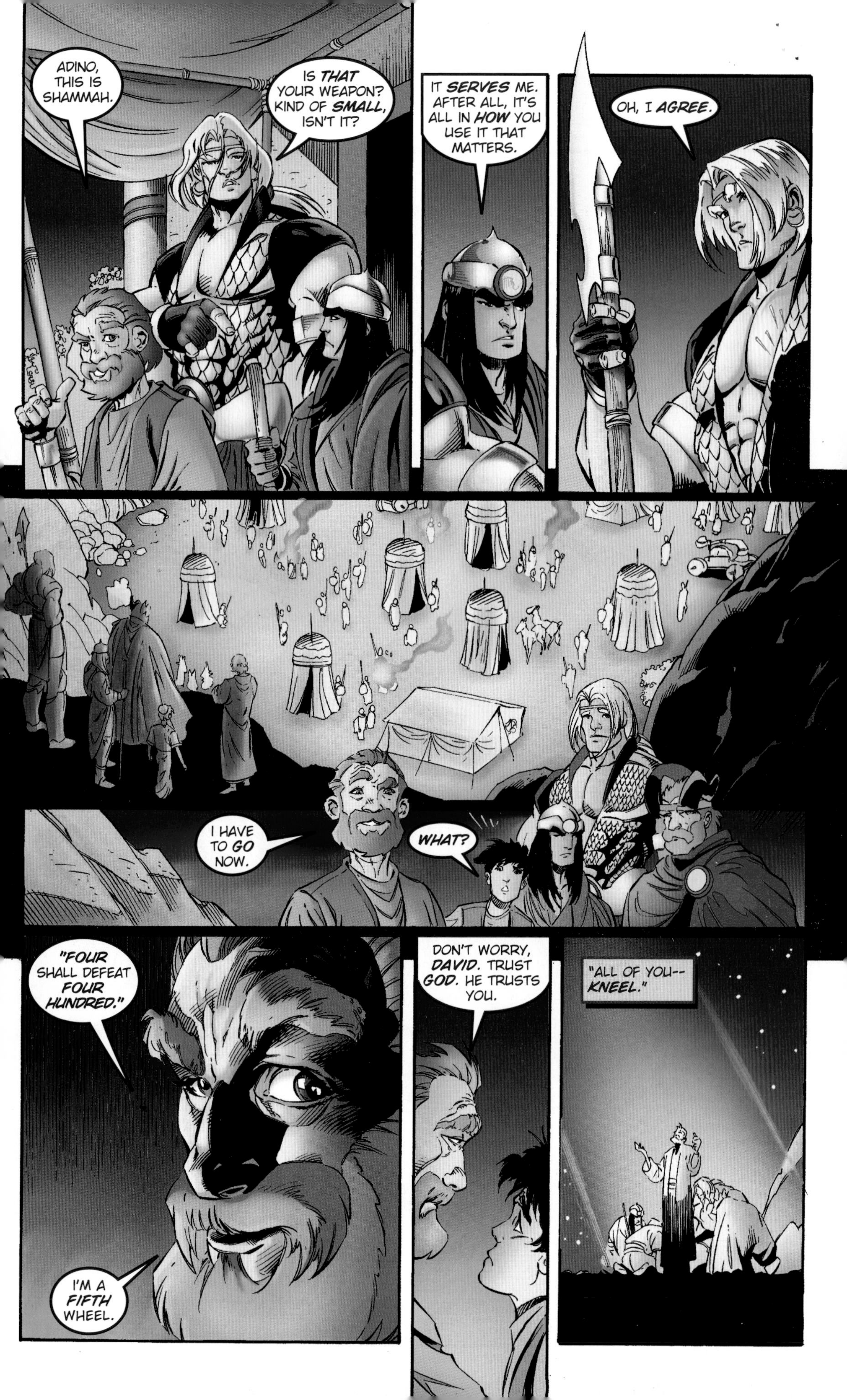
ADINO, THIS IS SHAMMAH.
IS THAT YOUR WEAPON? KIND OF SMALL, ISN'T IT?
IT SERVES ME. AFTER ALL, IT'S ALL IN HOW YOU USE IT THAT MATTERS.
OH, I AGREE.
I HAVE TO GO NOW.
WHAT?
"FOUR SHALL DEFEAT FOUR HUNDRED."
I'M A FIFTH WHEEL.
DON'T WORRY, DAVID. TRUST GOD. HE TRUSTS YOU.
"ALL OF YOU-- KNEEL."

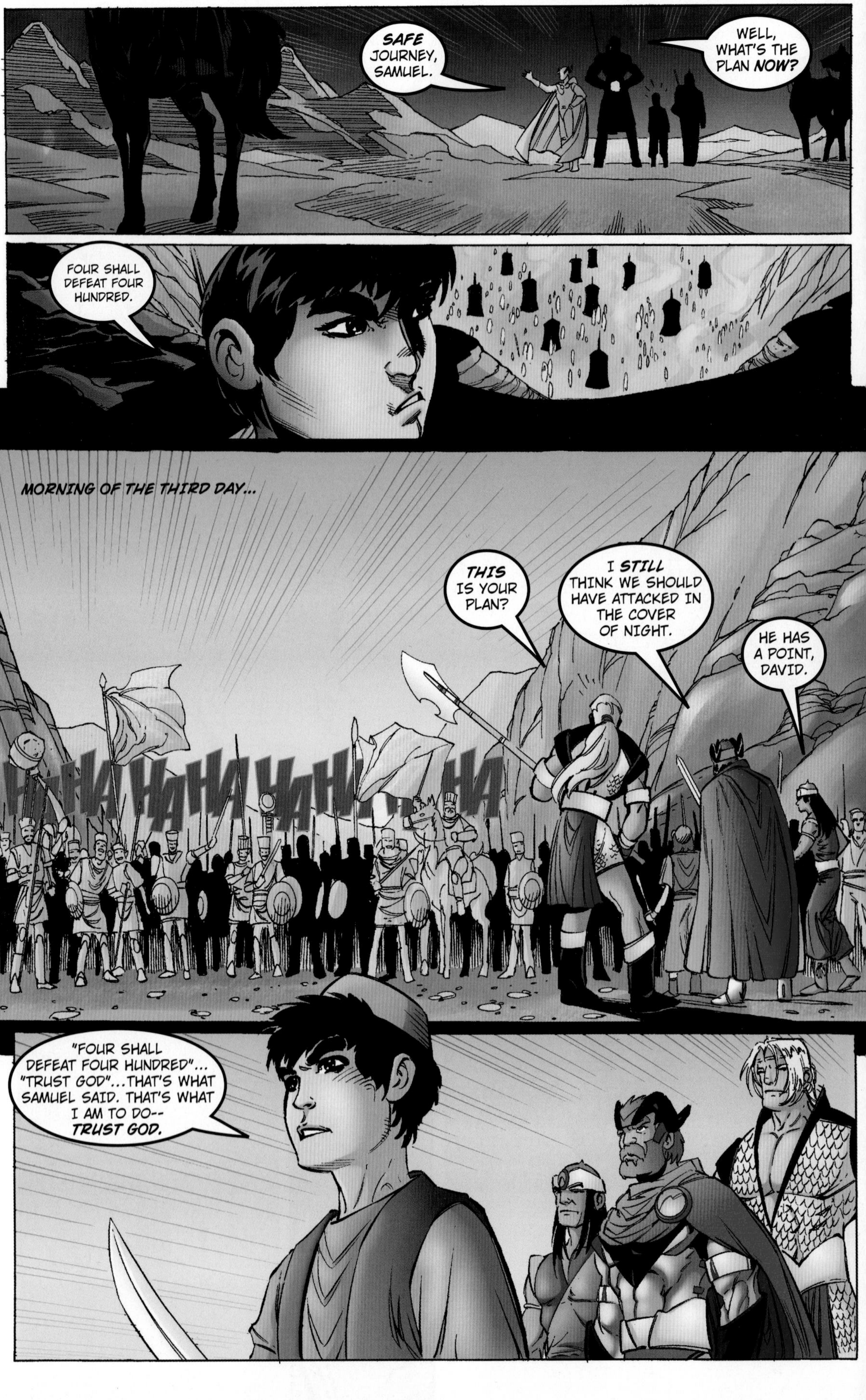
SAFE JOURNEY, SAMUEL.
WELL, WHAT'S THE PLAN NOW?
FOUR SHALL DEFEAT FOUR HUNDRED.
MORNING OF THE THIRD DAY...
THIS IS YOUR PLAN?
I STILL THINK WE SHOULD HAVE ATTACKED IN THE COVER OF NIGHT.
HE HAS A POINT, DAVID.
"FOUR SHALL DEFEAT FOUR HUNDRED"... "TRUST GOD"...THAT'S WHAT SAMUEL SAID. THAT'S WHAT I AM TO DO-- TRUST GOD.

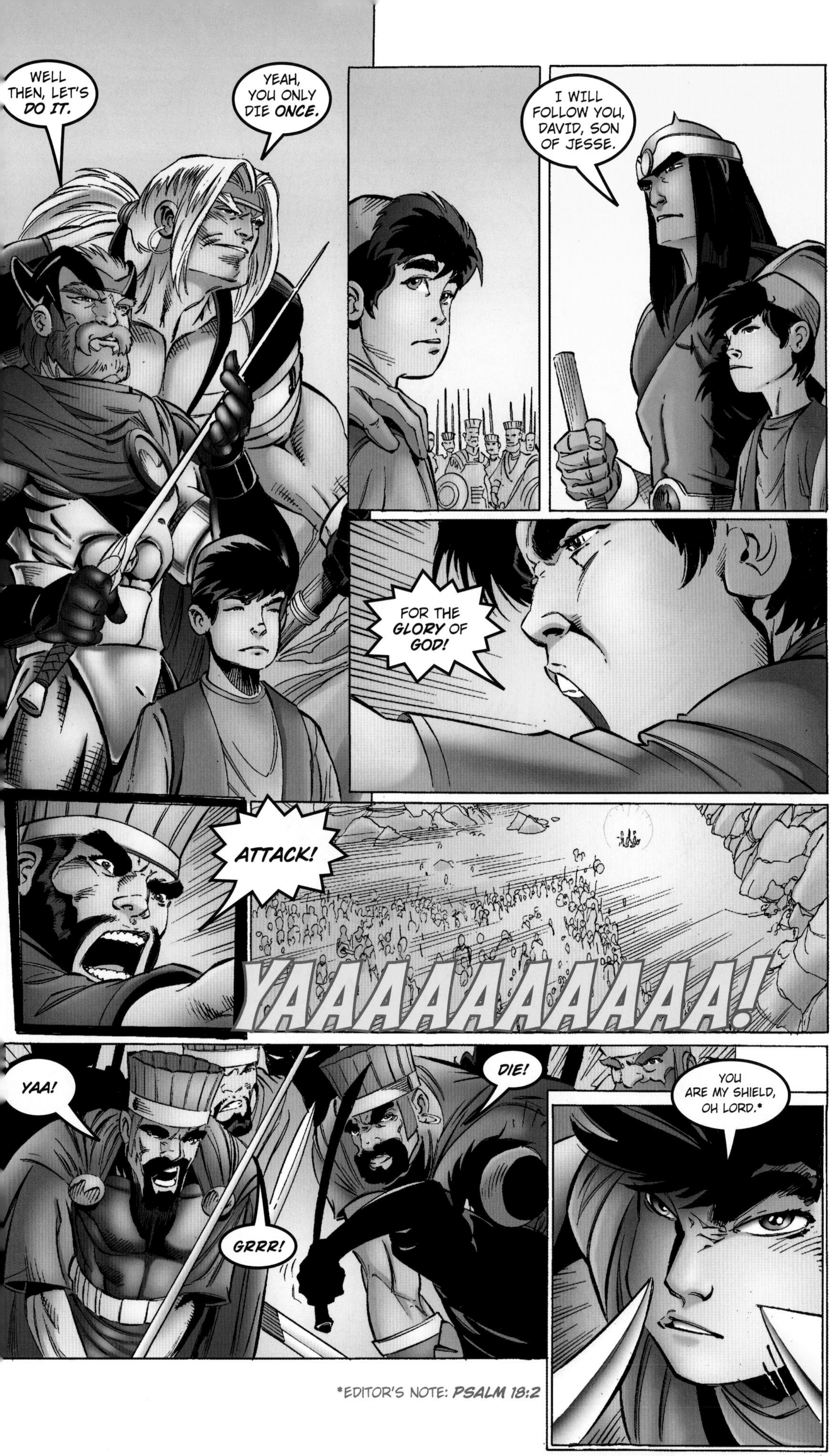
WELL THEN, LET'S DO IT.
YEAH, YOU ONLY DIE ONCE.
I WILL FOLLOW YOU, DAVID, SON OF JESSE.
FOR THE GLORY OF GOD!
ATTACK!
YAAAAAAAAAAA!
YAA!
GRRR!
DIE!
YOU ARE MY SHIELD, OH LORD.*

*EDITOR'S NOTE: PSALM 18:2

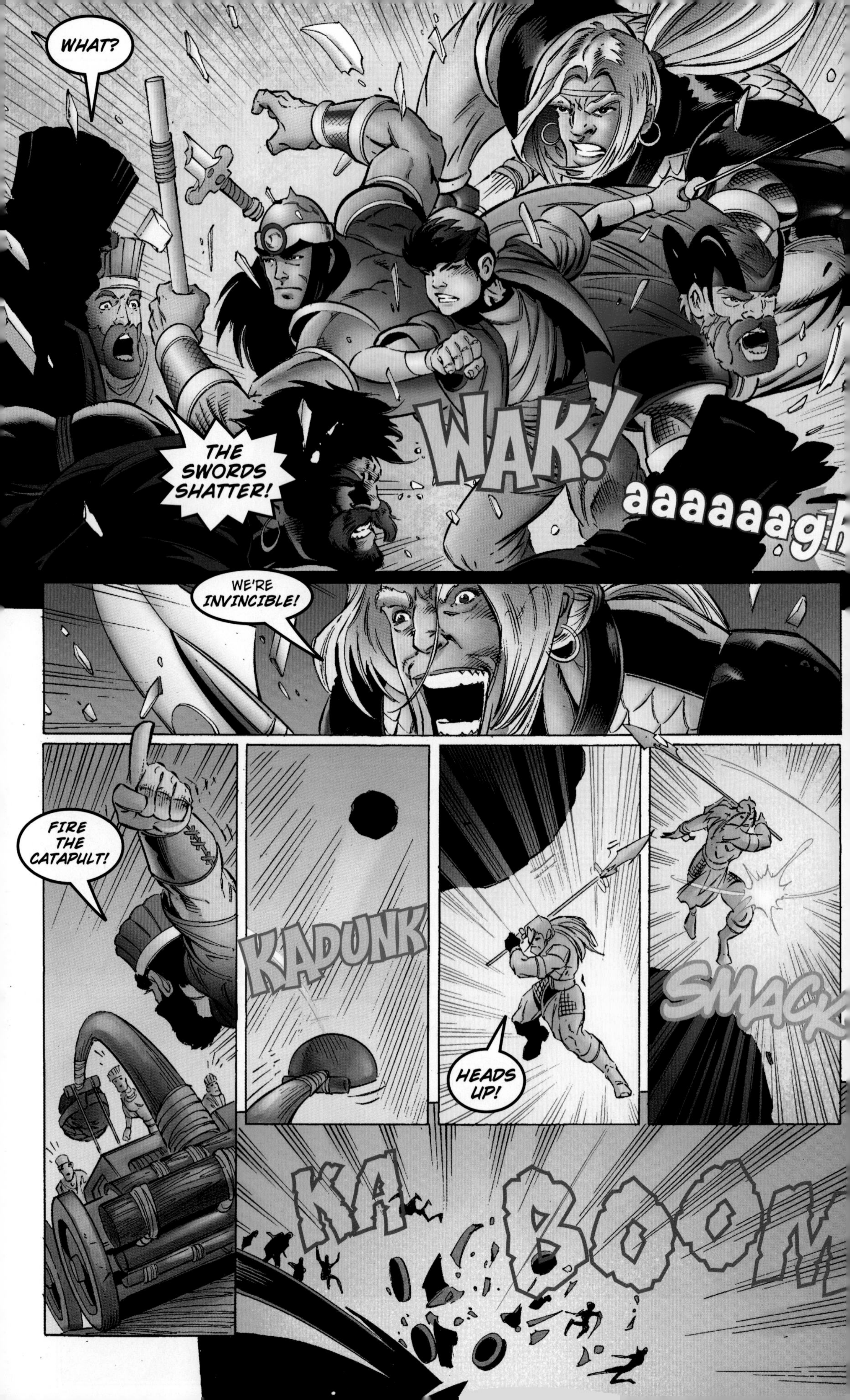
WHAT?
THE SWORDS SHATTER!
WAK!
aaaaaaagh
WE'RE INVINCIBLE!
FIRE THE CATAPULT!
KADUNK
HEADS UP!
SMACK
KA BOOM

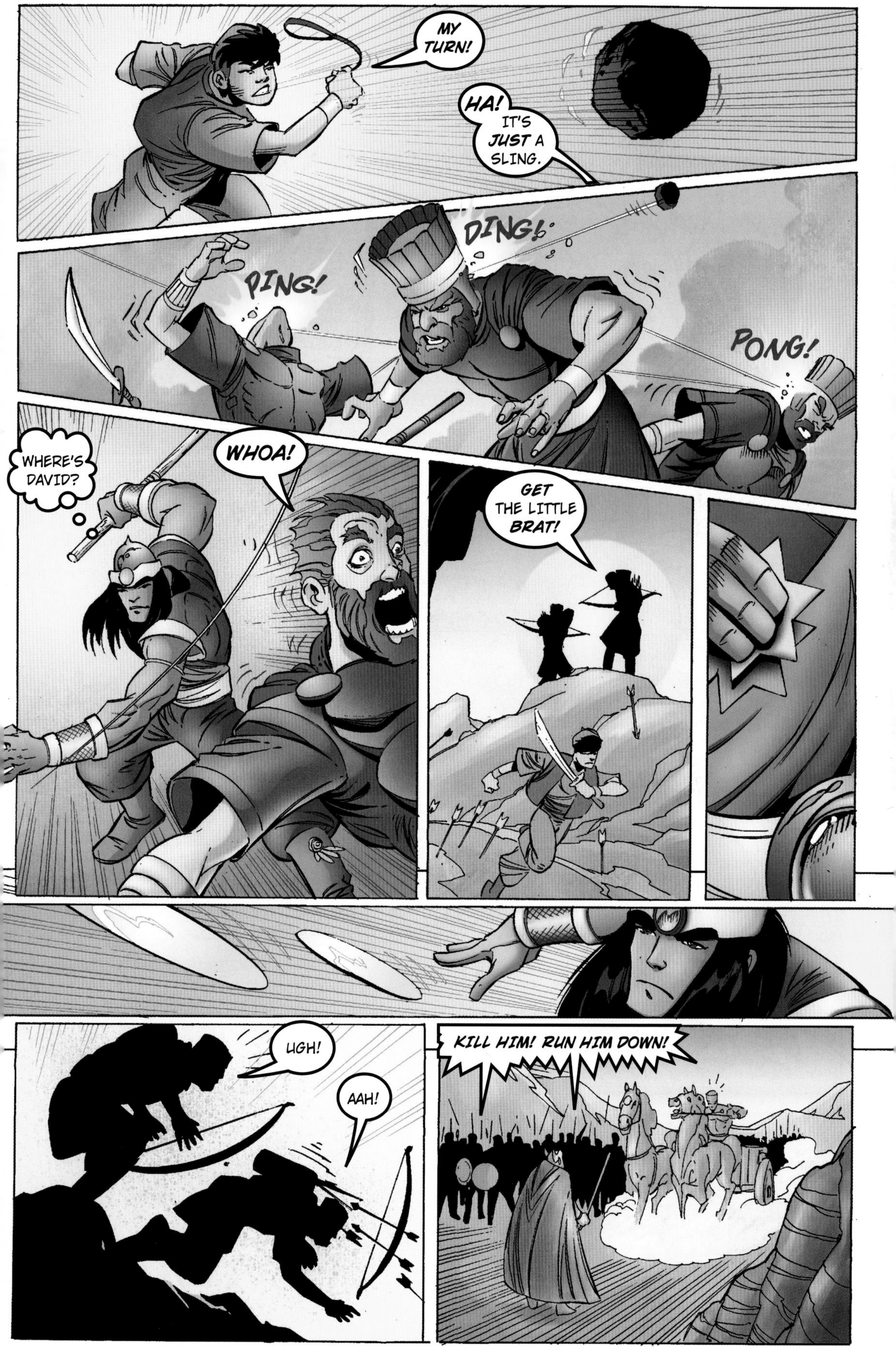
MY TURN!
HA! IT'S JUST A SLING.
DING!
PING!
PONG!
WHERE'S DAVID?
WHOA!
GET THE LITTLE BRAT!
UGH!
AAH!
KILL HIM! RUN HIM DOWN!

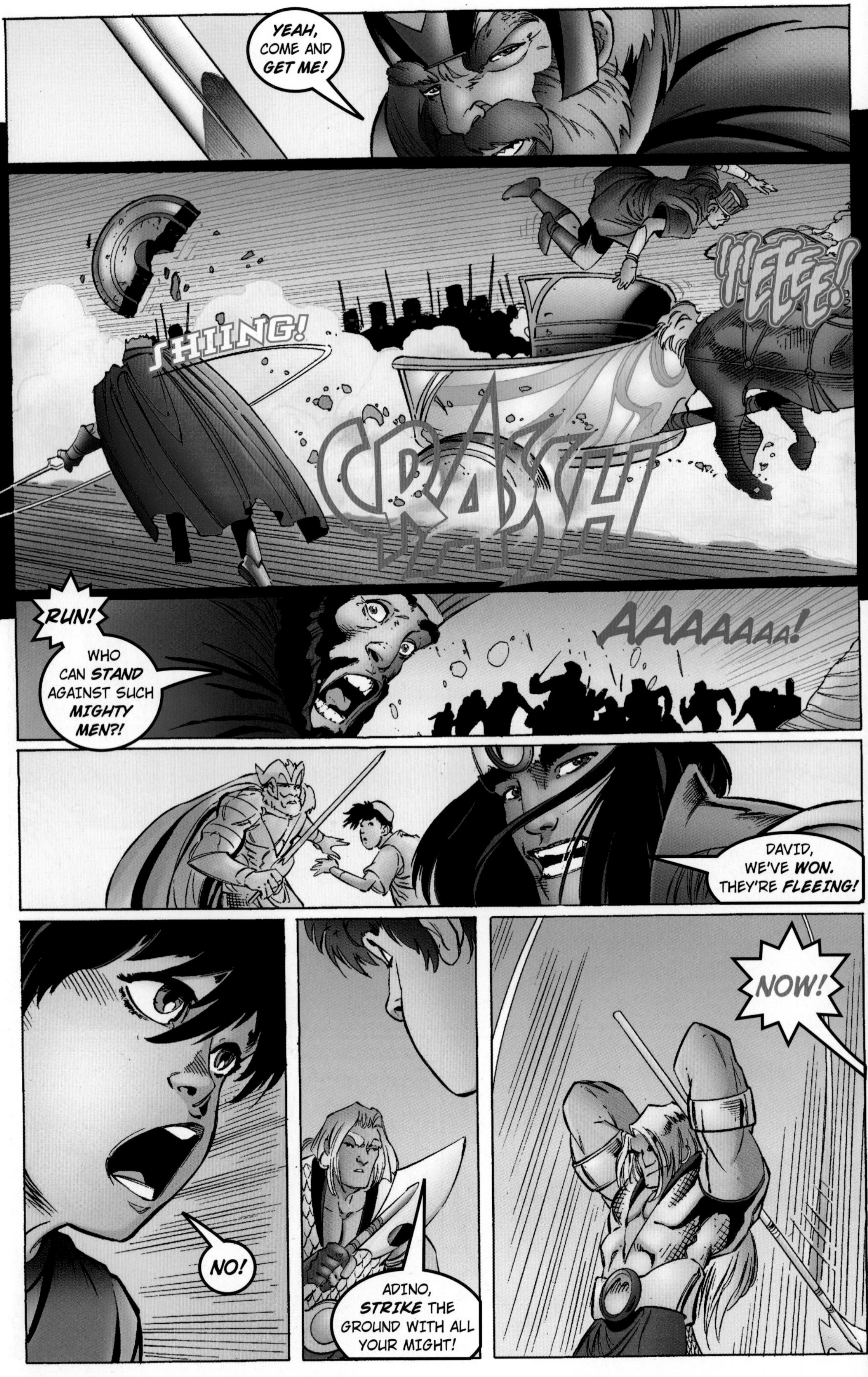
YEAH, COME AND GET ME!
SHIING!
YEEEE!
CRASH
RUN!
WHO CAN STAND AGAINST SUCH MIGHTY MEN?!
AAAAAAA!
DAVID, WE'VE WON. THEY'RE FLEEING!
NO!
ADINO, STRIKE THE GROUND WITH ALL YOUR MIGHT!
NOW!

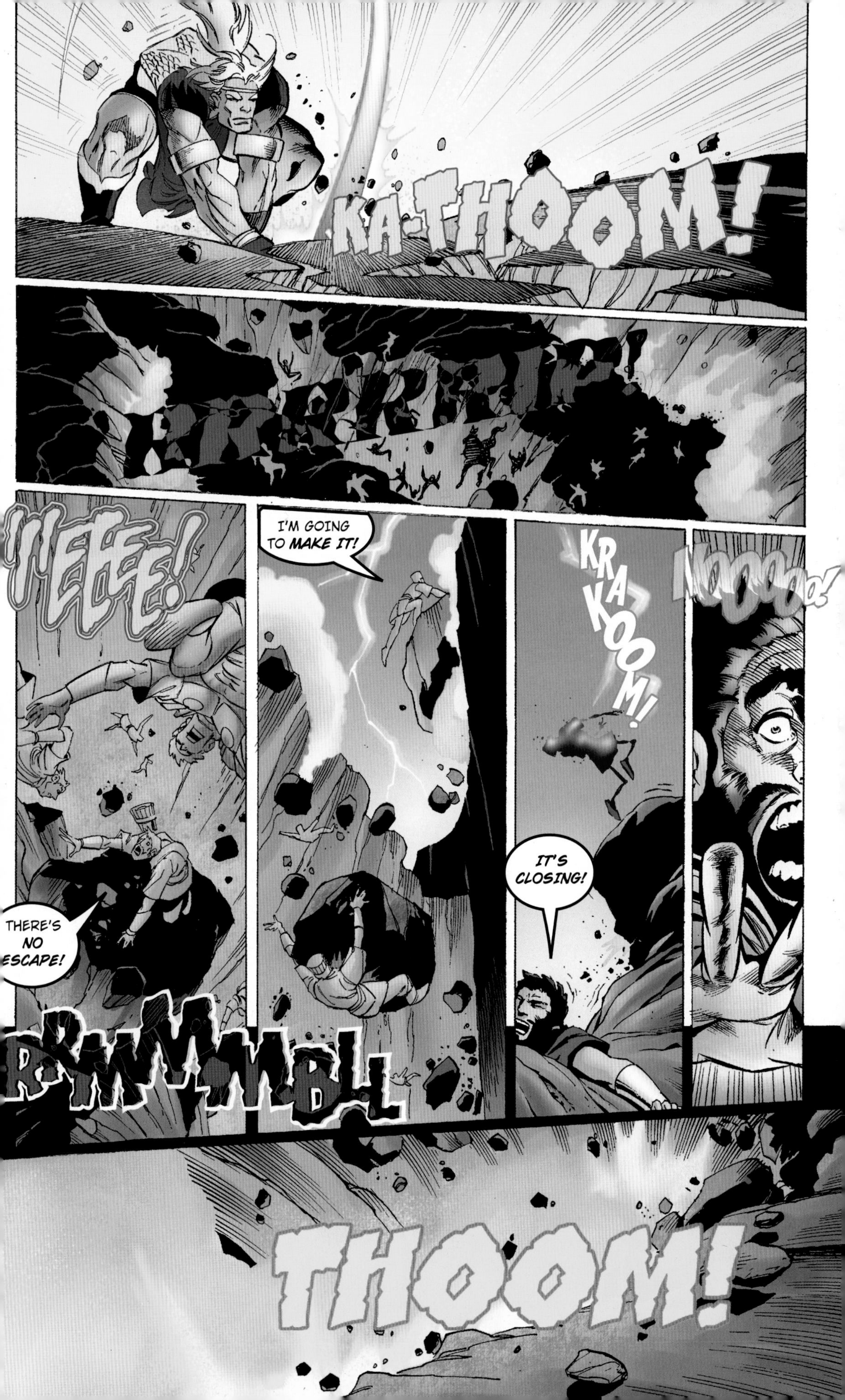
KA-THOOM!
THERE'S NO ESCAPE!
I'M GOING TO *MAKE IT!*
KRAKOOM!
IT'S CLOSING!
THOOM!

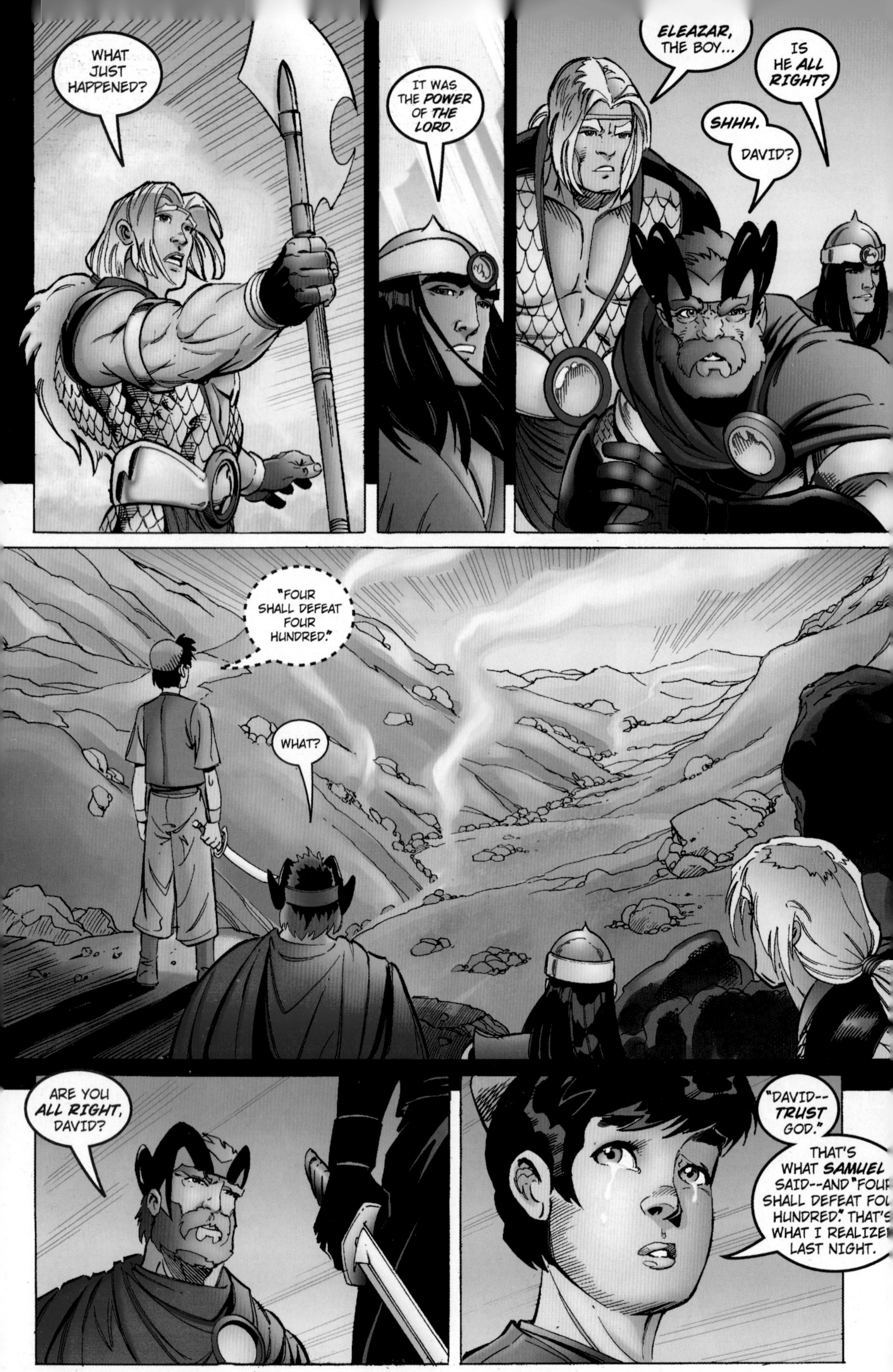
WHAT JUST HAPPENED?
IT WAS THE POWER OF THE LORD.
ELEAZAR, THE BOY...
IS HE ALL RIGHT?
SHHH.
DAVID?
"FOUR SHALL DEFEAT FOUR HUNDRED."
WHAT?
ARE YOU ALL RIGHT, DAVID?
"DAVID-- TRUST GOD."
THAT'S WHAT SAMUEL SAID--AND "FOUR SHALL DEFEAT FOU HUNDRED." THAT'S WHAT I REALIZE LAST NIGHT.

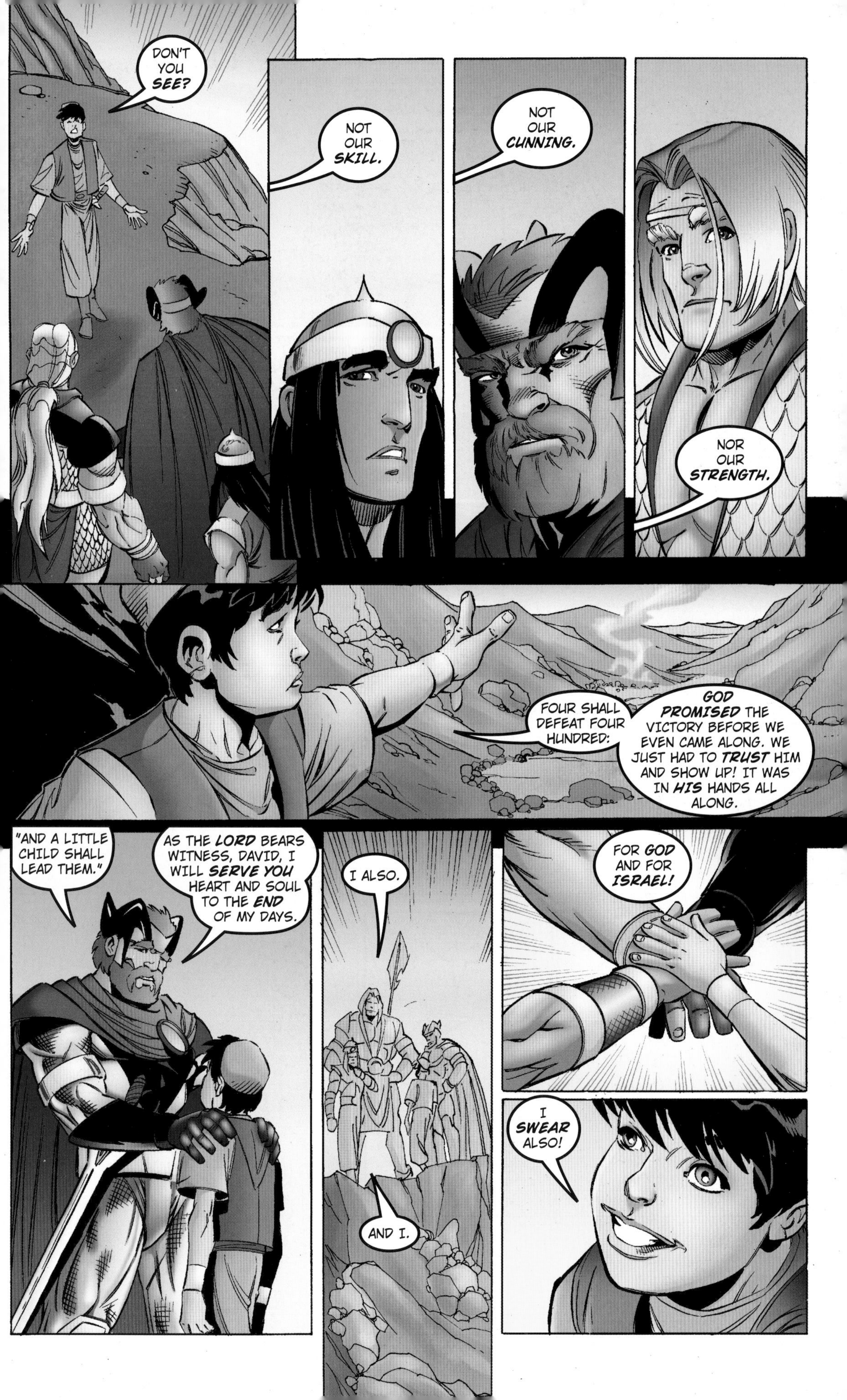
DON'T YOU SEE?
NOT OUR SKILL.
NOT OUR CUNNING.
NOR OUR STRENGTH.
FOUR SHALL DEFEAT FOUR HUNDRED:
GOD PROMISED THE VICTORY BEFORE WE EVEN CAME ALONG. WE JUST HAD TO TRUST HIM AND SHOW UP! IT WAS IN HIS HANDS ALL ALONG.
"AND A LITTLE CHILD SHALL LEAD THEM."
AS THE LORD BEARS WITNESS, DAVID, I WILL SERVE YOU HEART AND SOUL TO THE END OF MY DAYS.
I ALSO.
AND I.
FOR GOD AND FOR ISRAEL!
I SWEAR ALSO!

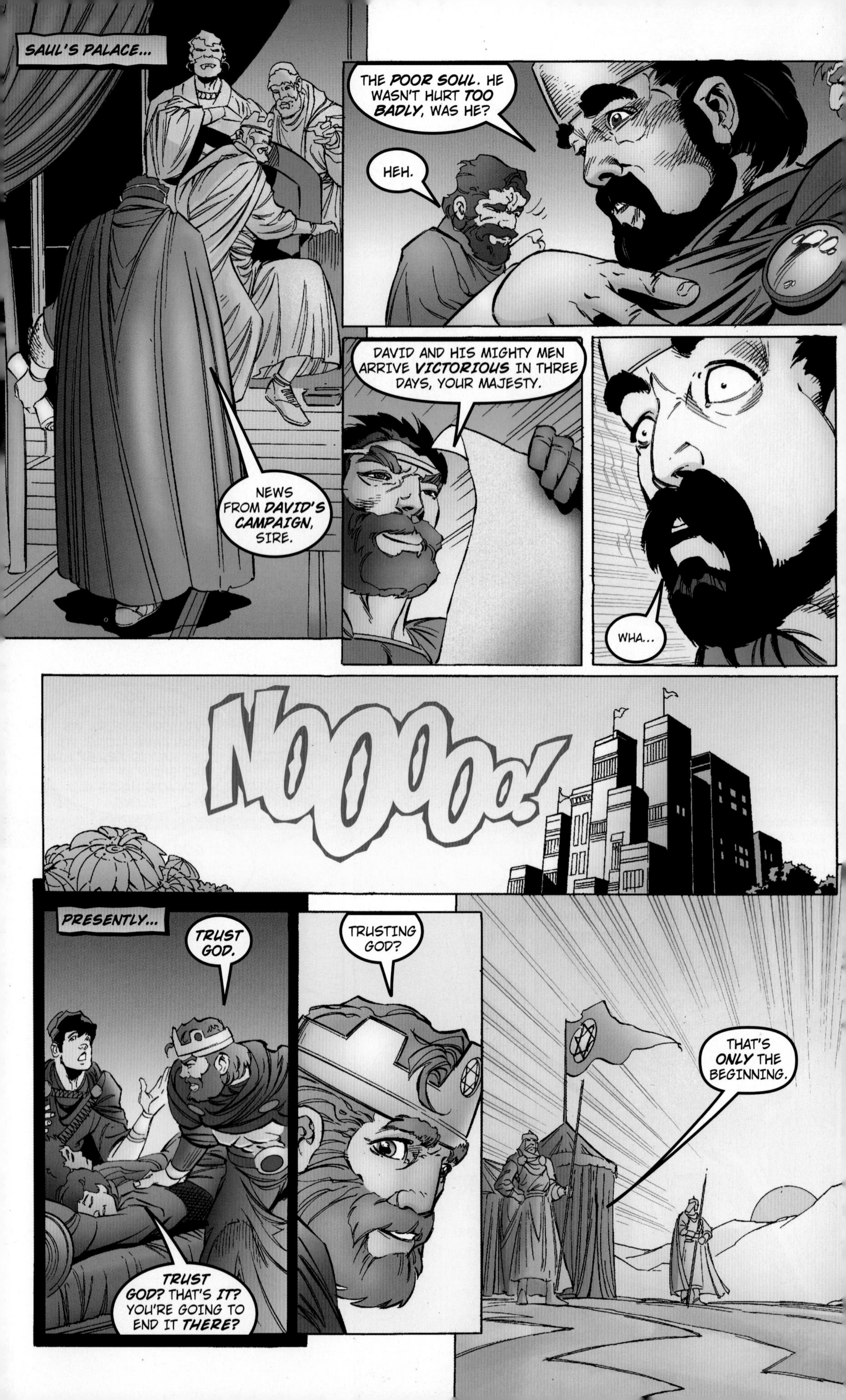
SAUL'S PALACE...
NEWS FROM DAVID'S CAMPAIGN, SIRE.
THE POOR SOUL. HE WASN'T HURT TOO BADLY, WAS HE?
HEH.
DAVID AND HIS MIGHTY MEN ARRIVE VICTORIOUS IN THREE DAYS, YOUR MAJESTY.
WHA...
NOOOOO!
PRESENTLY...
TRUST GOD.
TRUST GOD? THAT'S IT? YOU'RE GOING TO END IT THERE?
TRUSTING GOD?
THAT'S ONLY THE BEGINNING.

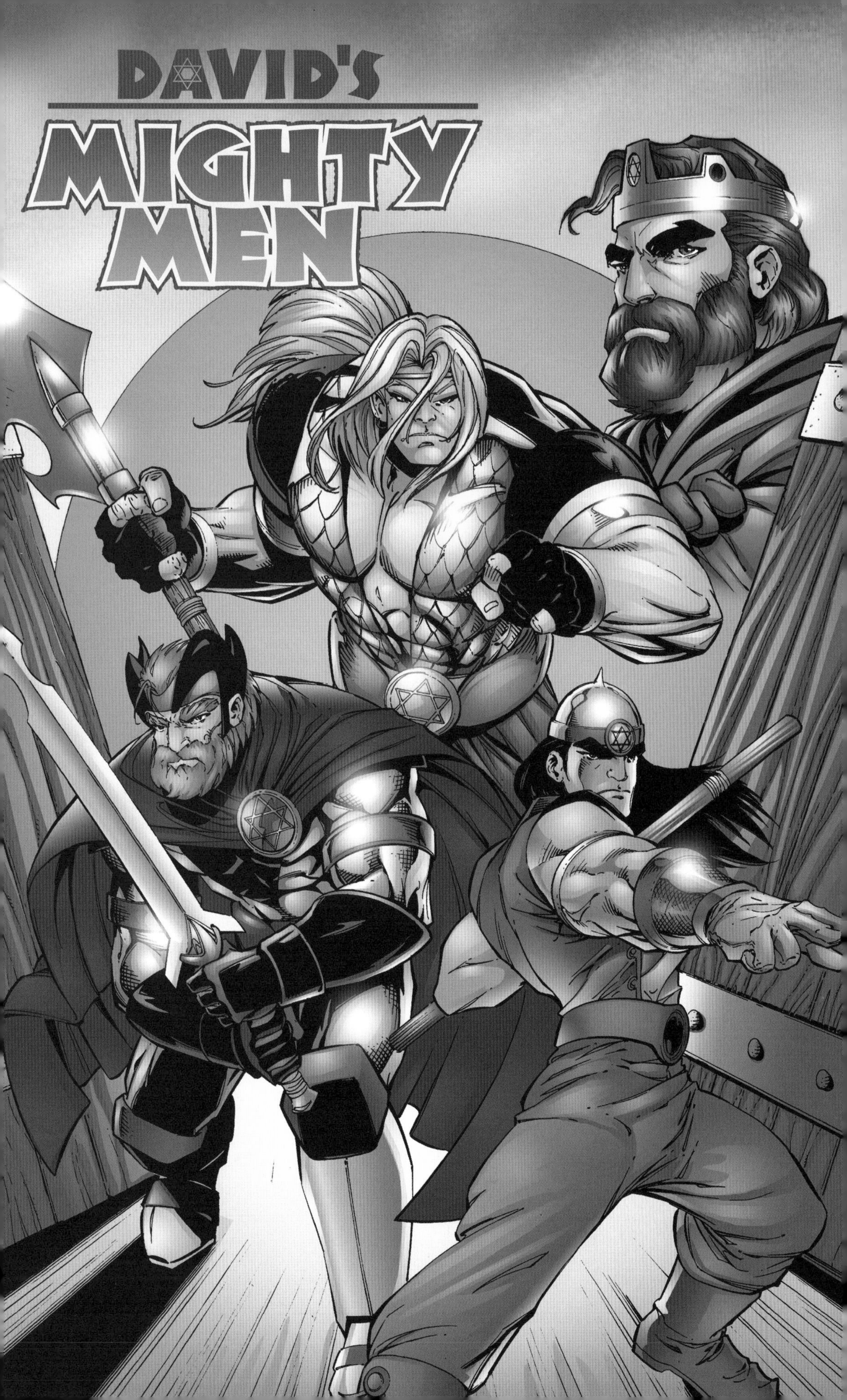
DAVID'S
MIGHTY
MEN

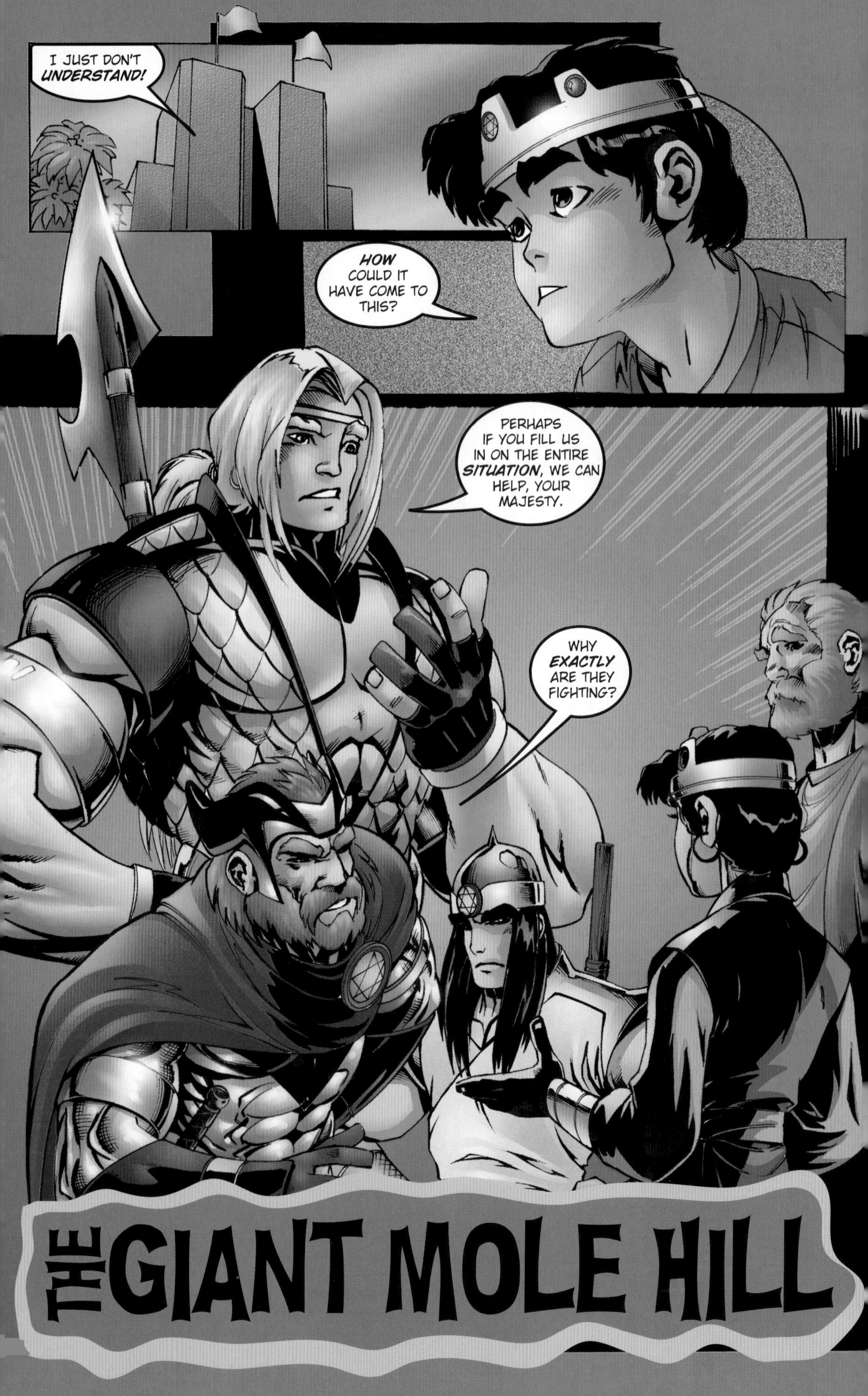

I JUST DON'T UNDERSTAND!
HOW COULD IT HAVE COME TO THIS?
PERHAPS IF YOU FILL US IN ON THE ENTIRE SITUATION, WE CAN HELP, YOUR MAJESTY.
WHY EXACTLY ARE THEY FIGHTING?
THE GIANT MOLE HILL

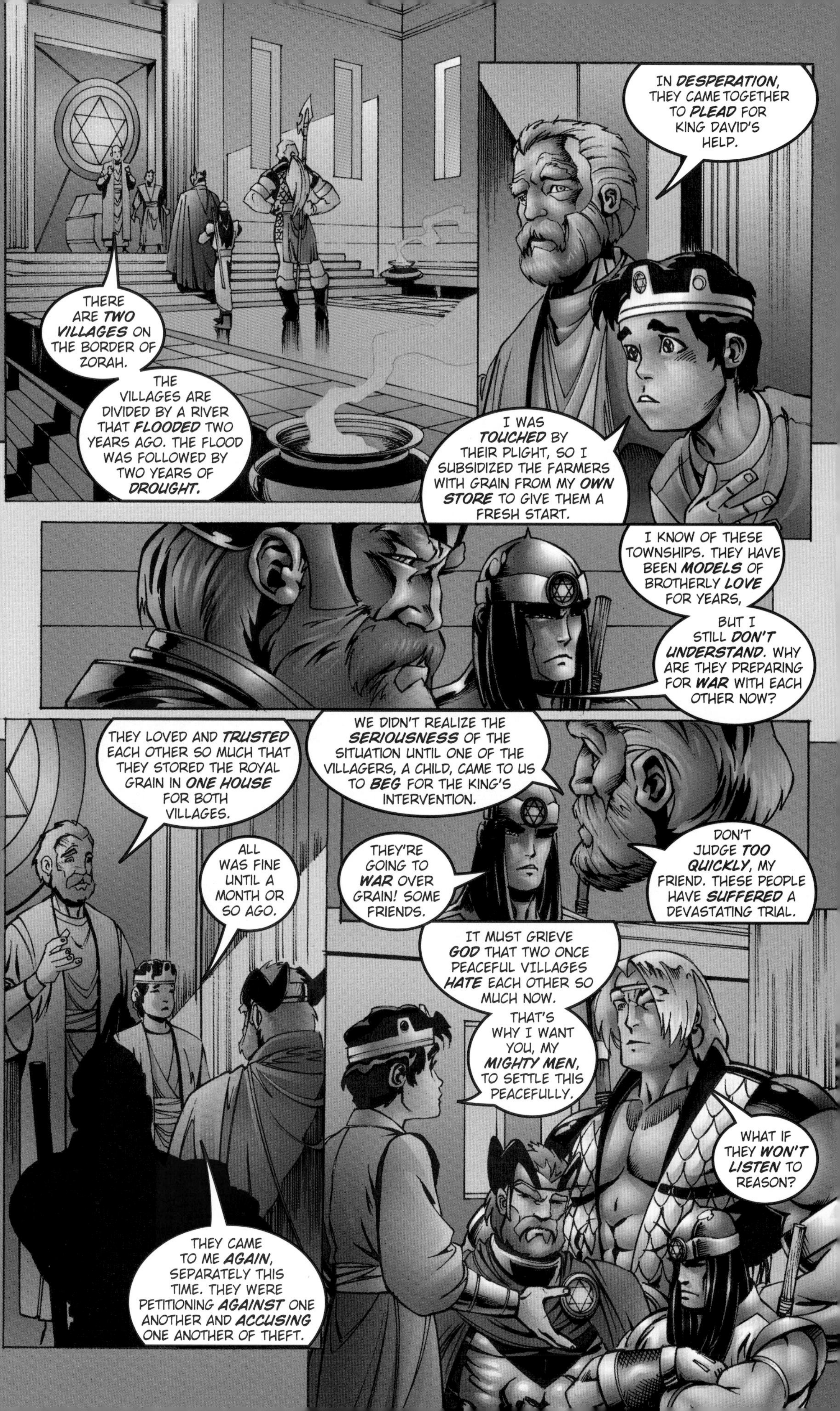
THERE ARE TWO VILLAGES ON THE BORDER OF ZORAH.
THE VILLAGES ARE DIVIDED BY A RIVER THAT FLOODED TWO YEARS AGO. THE FLOOD WAS FOLLOWED BY TWO YEARS OF DROUGHT.
IN DESPERATION, THEY CAME TOGETHER TO PLEAD FOR KING DAVID'S HELP.
I WAS TOUCHED BY THEIR PLIGHT, SO I SUBSIDIZED THE FARMERS WITH GRAIN FROM MY OWN STORE TO GIVE THEM A FRESH START.
I KNOW OF THESE TOWNSHIPS. THEY HAVE BEEN MODELS OF BROTHERLY LOVE FOR YEARS,
BUT I STILL DON'T UNDERSTAND. WHY ARE THEY PREPARING FOR WAR WITH EACH OTHER NOW?
THEY LOVED AND TRUSTED EACH OTHER SO MUCH THAT THEY STORED THE ROYAL GRAIN IN ONE HOUSE FOR BOTH VILLAGES.
ALL WAS FINE UNTIL A MONTH OR SO AGO.
THEY CAME TO ME AGAIN, SEPARATELY THIS TIME. THEY WERE PETITIONING AGAINST ONE ANOTHER AND ACCUSING ONE ANOTHER OF THEFT.
WE DIDN'T REALIZE THE SERIOUSNESS OF THE SITUATION UNTIL ONE OF THE VILLAGERS, A CHILD, CAME TO US TO BEG FOR THE KING'S INTERVENTION.
THEY'RE GOING TO WAR OVER GRAIN! SOME FRIENDS.
DON'T JUDGE TOO QUICKLY, MY FRIEND. THESE PEOPLE HAVE SUFFERED A DEVASTATING TRIAL.
IT MUST GRIEVE GOD THAT TWO ONCE PEACEFUL VILLAGES HATE EACH OTHER SO MUCH NOW.
THAT'S WHY I WANT YOU, MY MIGHTY MEN, TO SETTLE THIS PEACEFULLY.
WHAT IF THEY WON'T LISTEN TO REASON?

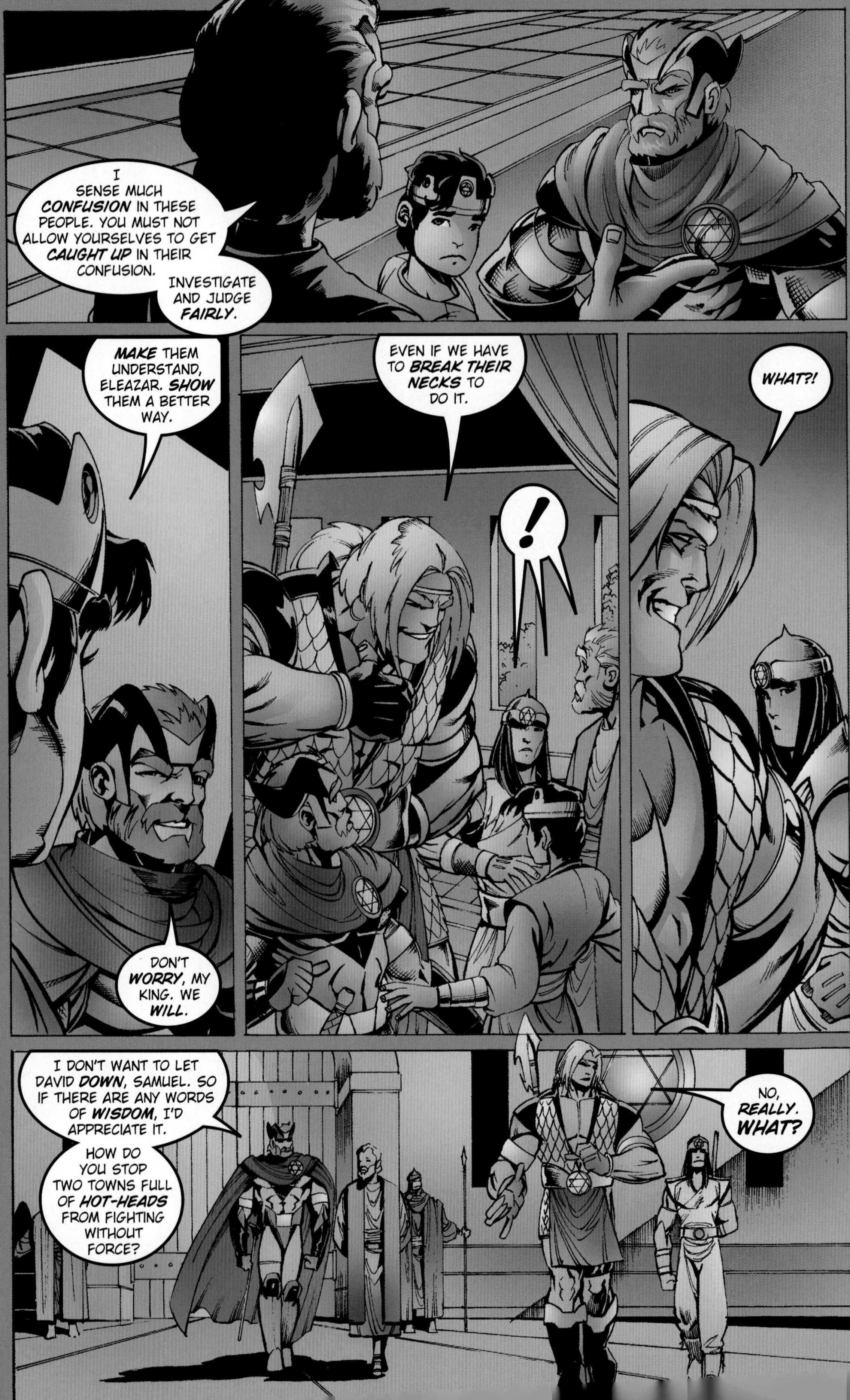
I SENSE MUCH CONFUSION IN THESE PEOPLE. YOU MUST NOT ALLOW YOURSELVES TO GET CAUGHT UP IN THEIR CONFUSION.
INVESTIGATE AND JUDGE FAIRLY.
MAKE THEM UNDERSTAND, ELEAZAR. SHOW THEM A BETTER WAY.
DON'T WORRY, MY KING. WE WILL.
EVEN IF WE HAVE TO BREAK THEIR NECKS TO DO IT.
!
WHAT?!
I DON'T WANT TO LET DAVID DOWN, SAMUEL. SO IF THERE ARE ANY WORDS OF WISDOM, I'D APPRECIATE IT.
HOW DO YOU STOP TWO TOWNS FULL OF HOT-HEADS FROM FIGHTING WITHOUT FORCE?
NO, REALLY. WHAT?

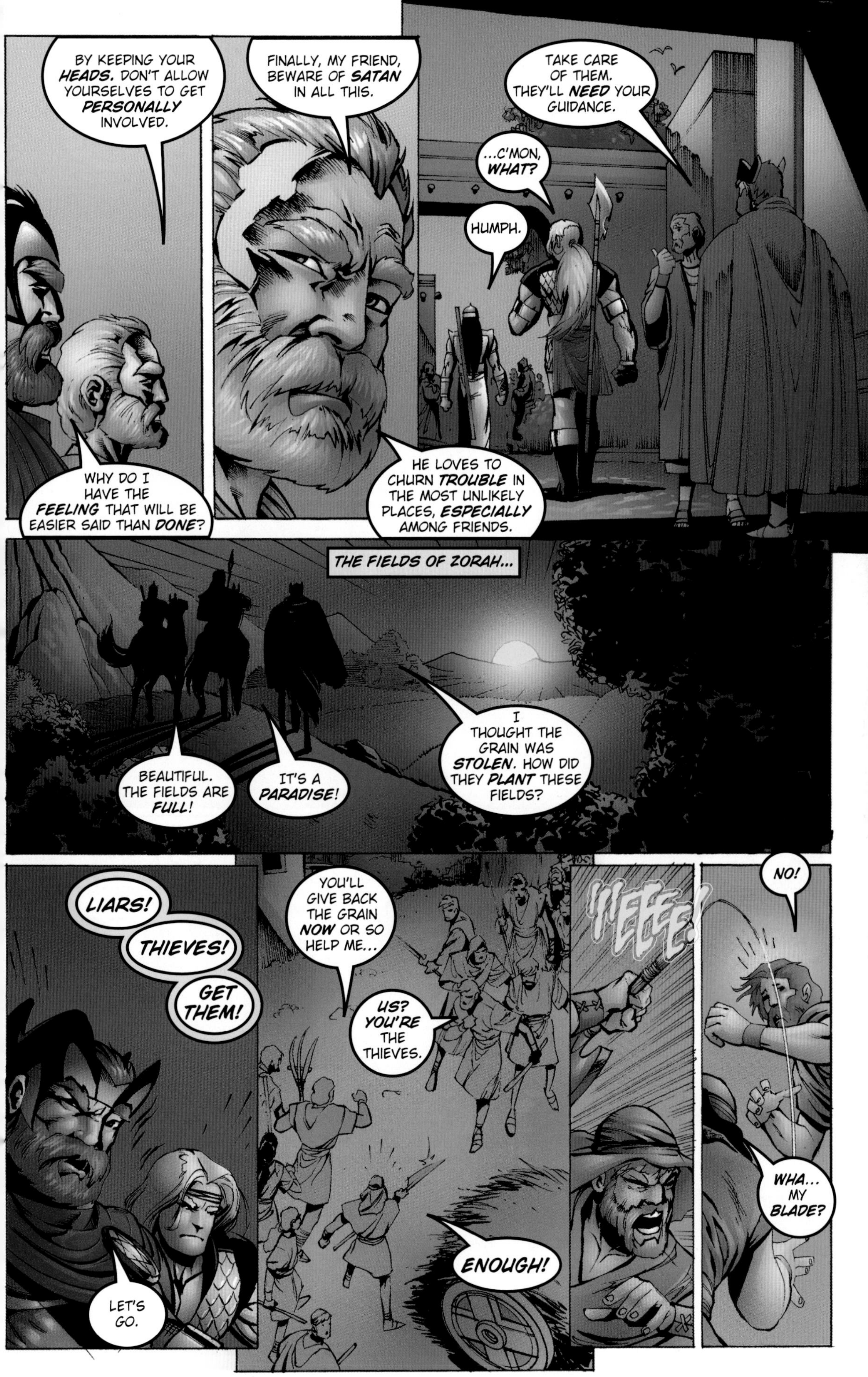
BY KEEPING YOUR HEADS. DON'T ALLOW YOURSELVES TO GET PERSONALLY INVOLVED.
WHY DO I HAVE THE FEELING THAT WILL BE EASIER SAID THAN DONE?
FINALLY, MY FRIEND, BEWARE OF SATAN IN ALL THIS.
HE LOVES TO CHURN TROUBLE IN THE MOST UNLIKELY PLACES, ESPECIALLY AMONG FRIENDS.
TAKE CARE OF THEM. THEY'LL NEED YOUR GUIDANCE.
...C'MON, WHAT?
HUMPH.
THE FIELDS OF ZORAH...
BEAUTIFUL. THE FIELDS ARE FULL!
IT'S A PARADISE!
I THOUGHT THE GRAIN WAS STOLEN. HOW DID THEY PLANT THESE FIELDS?
LIARS!
THIEVES!
GET THEM!
LET'S GO.
YOU'LL GIVE BACK THE GRAIN NOW OR SO HELP ME...
US? YOU'RE THE THIEVES.
ENOUGH!
NO!
WHA... MY BLADE?

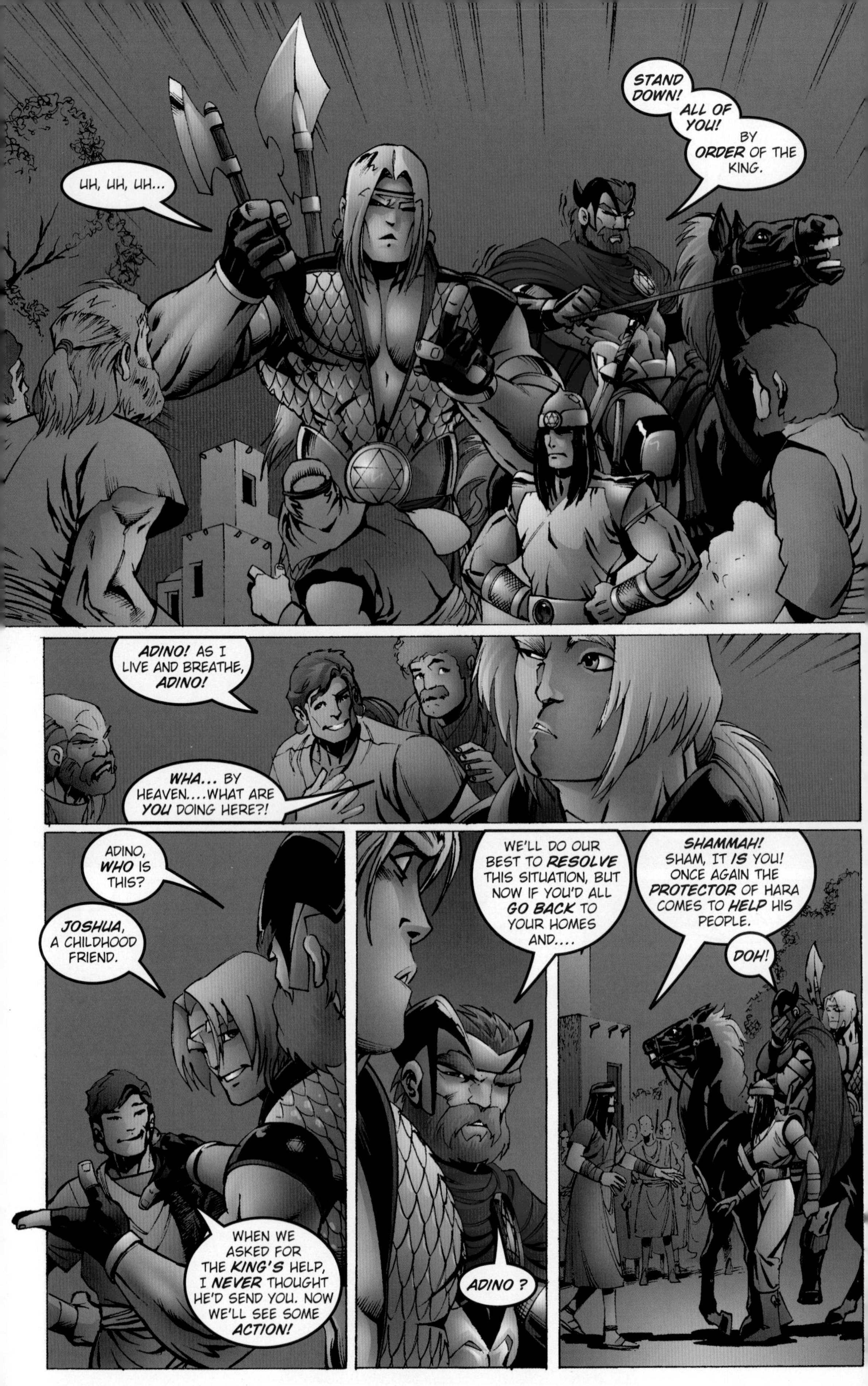
UH, UH, UH...
STAND DOWN! ALL OF YOU! BY ORDER OF THE KING.
ADINO! AS I LIVE AND BREATHE, ADINO!
WHA... BY HEAVEN....WHAT ARE YOU DOING HERE?!
ADINO, WHO IS THIS?
JOSHUA, A CHILDHOOD FRIEND.
WHEN WE ASKED FOR THE KING'S HELP, I NEVER THOUGHT HE'D SEND YOU. NOW WE'LL SEE SOME ACTION!
WE'LL DO OUR BEST TO RESOLVE THIS SITUATION, BUT NOW IF YOU'D ALL GO BACK TO YOUR HOMES AND....
ADINO ?
SHAMMAH! SHAM, IT IS YOU! ONCE AGAIN THE PROTECTOR OF HARA COMES TO HELP HIS PEOPLE.
DOH!

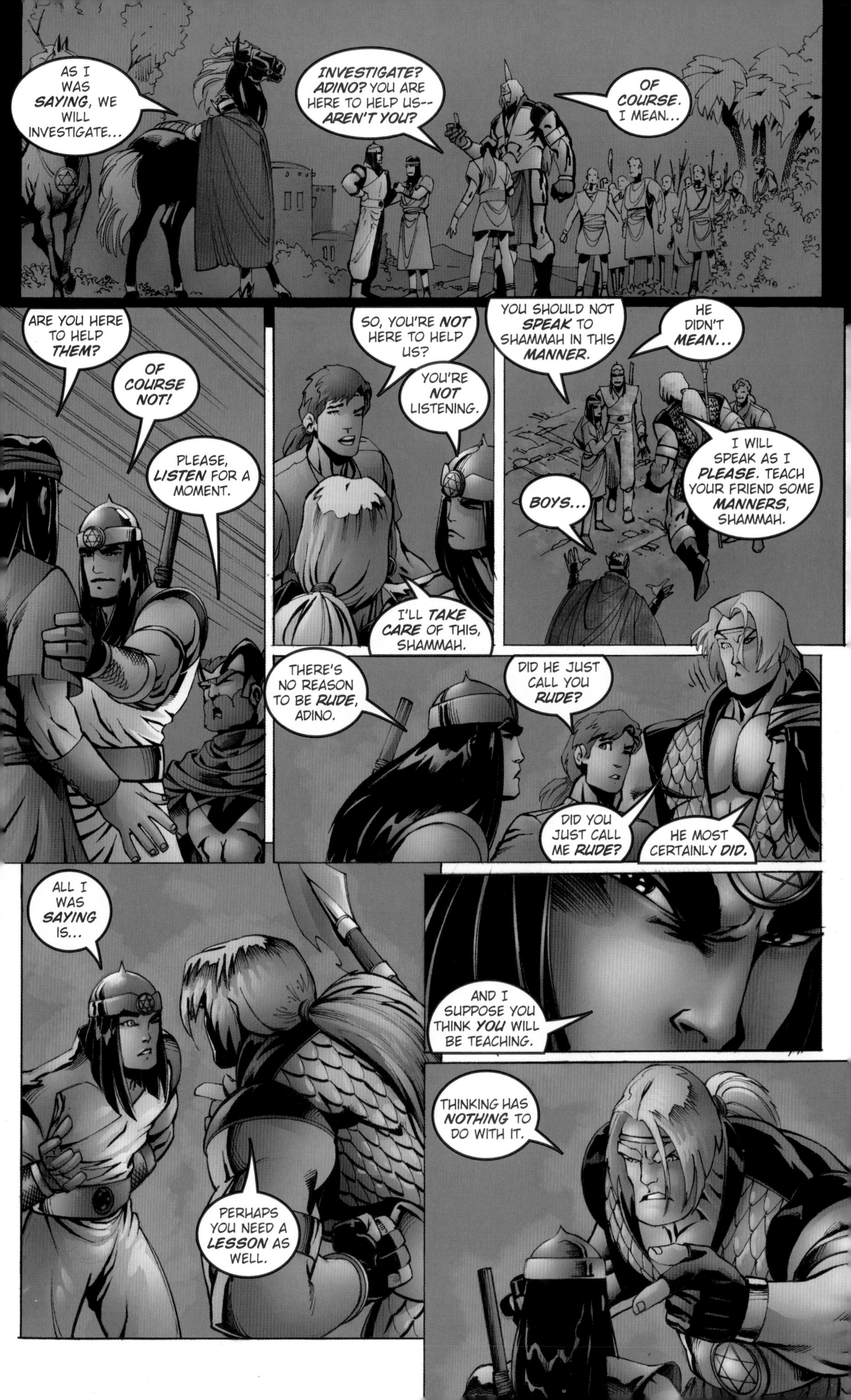
AS I WAS SAYING, WE WILL INVESTIGATE...
INVESTIGATE? ADINO? YOU ARE HERE TO HELP US-- AREN'T YOU?
OF COURSE. I MEAN...
ARE YOU HERE TO HELP THEM?
OF COURSE NOT!
PLEASE, LISTEN FOR A MOMENT.
SO, YOU'RE NOT HERE TO HELP US?
YOU'RE NOT LISTENING.
I'LL TAKE CARE OF THIS, SHAMMAH.
YOU SHOULD NOT SPEAK TO SHAMMAH IN THIS MANNER.
HE DIDN'T MEAN...
I WILL SPEAK AS I PLEASE. TEACH YOUR FRIEND SOME MANNERS, SHAMMAH.
BOYS...
THERE'S NO REASON TO BE RUDE, ADINO.
DID HE JUST CALL YOU RUDE?
DID YOU JUST CALL ME RUDE?
HE MOST CERTAINLY DID.
ALL I WAS SAYING IS...
PERHAPS YOU NEED A LESSON AS WELL.
AND I SUPPOSE YOU THINK YOU WILL BE TEACHING.
THINKING HAS NOTHING TO DO WITH IT.

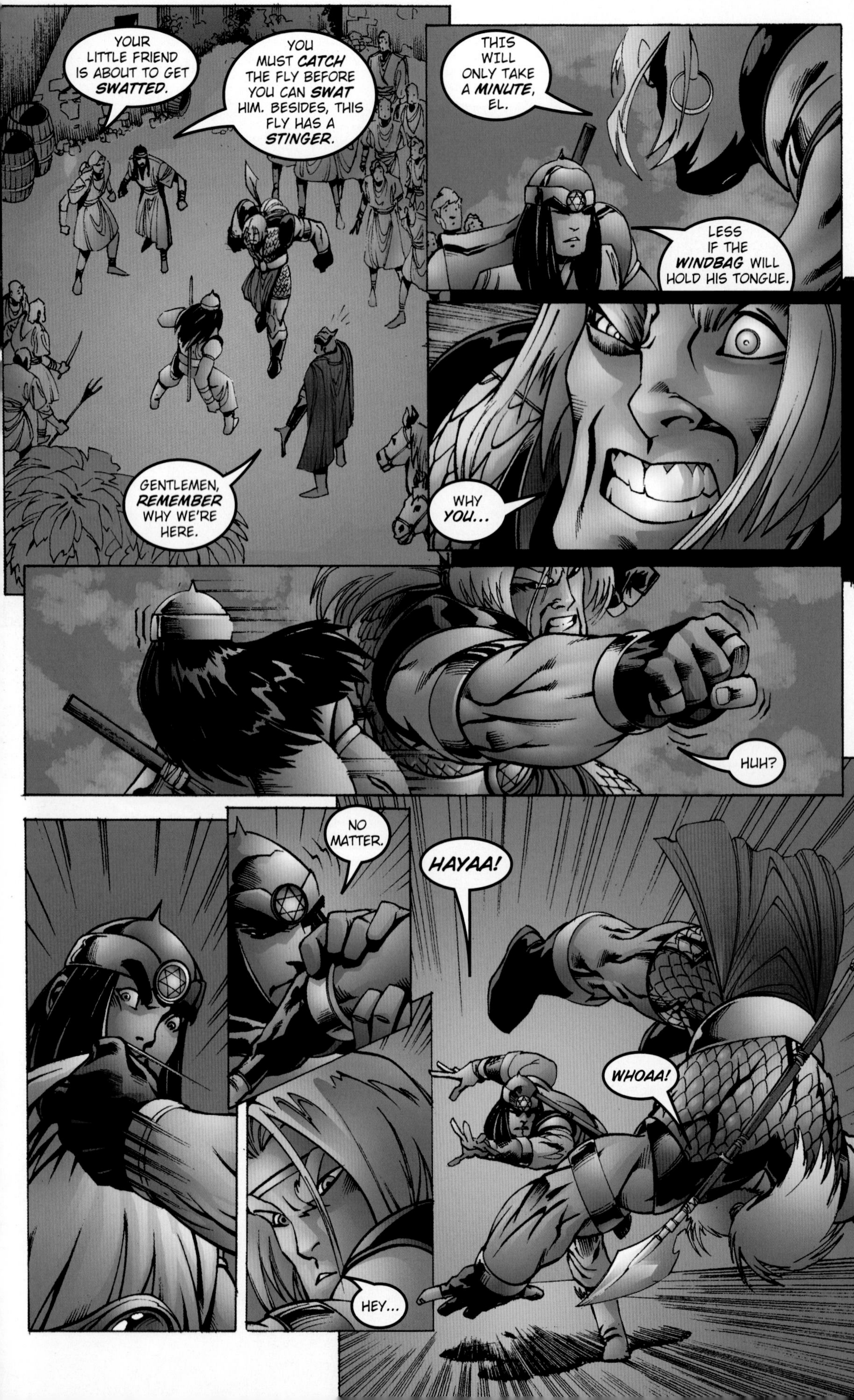
YOUR LITTLE FRIEND IS ABOUT TO GET SWATTED.
YOU MUST CATCH THE FLY BEFORE YOU CAN SWAT HIM. BESIDES, THIS FLY HAS A STINGER.
GENTLEMEN, REMEMBER WHY WE'RE HERE.
THIS WILL ONLY TAKE A MINUTE, EL.
LESS IF THE WINDBAG WILL HOLD HIS TONGUE.
WHY YOU...
HUH?
NO MATTER.
HEY...
HAYAA!
WHOAA!

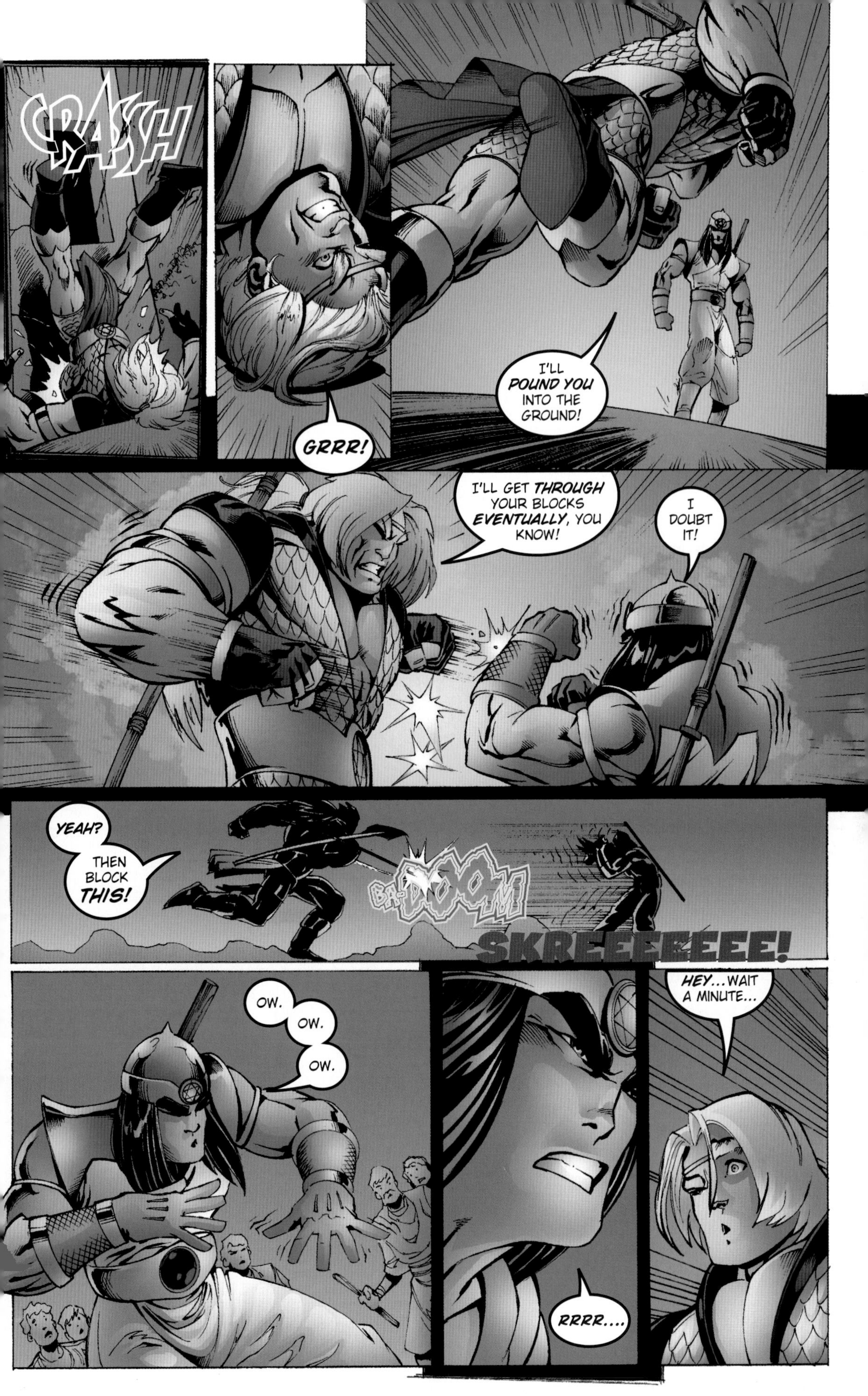
CRASH
GRRR!
I'LL POUND YOU INTO THE GROUND!
I'LL GET THROUGH YOUR BLOCKS EVENTUALLY, YOU KNOW!
I DOUBT IT!
YEAH?
THEN BLOCK THIS!
BA-DOOM
SKREEEEEEEE!
OW.
OW.
OW.
RRRR....
HEY...WAIT A MINUTE...

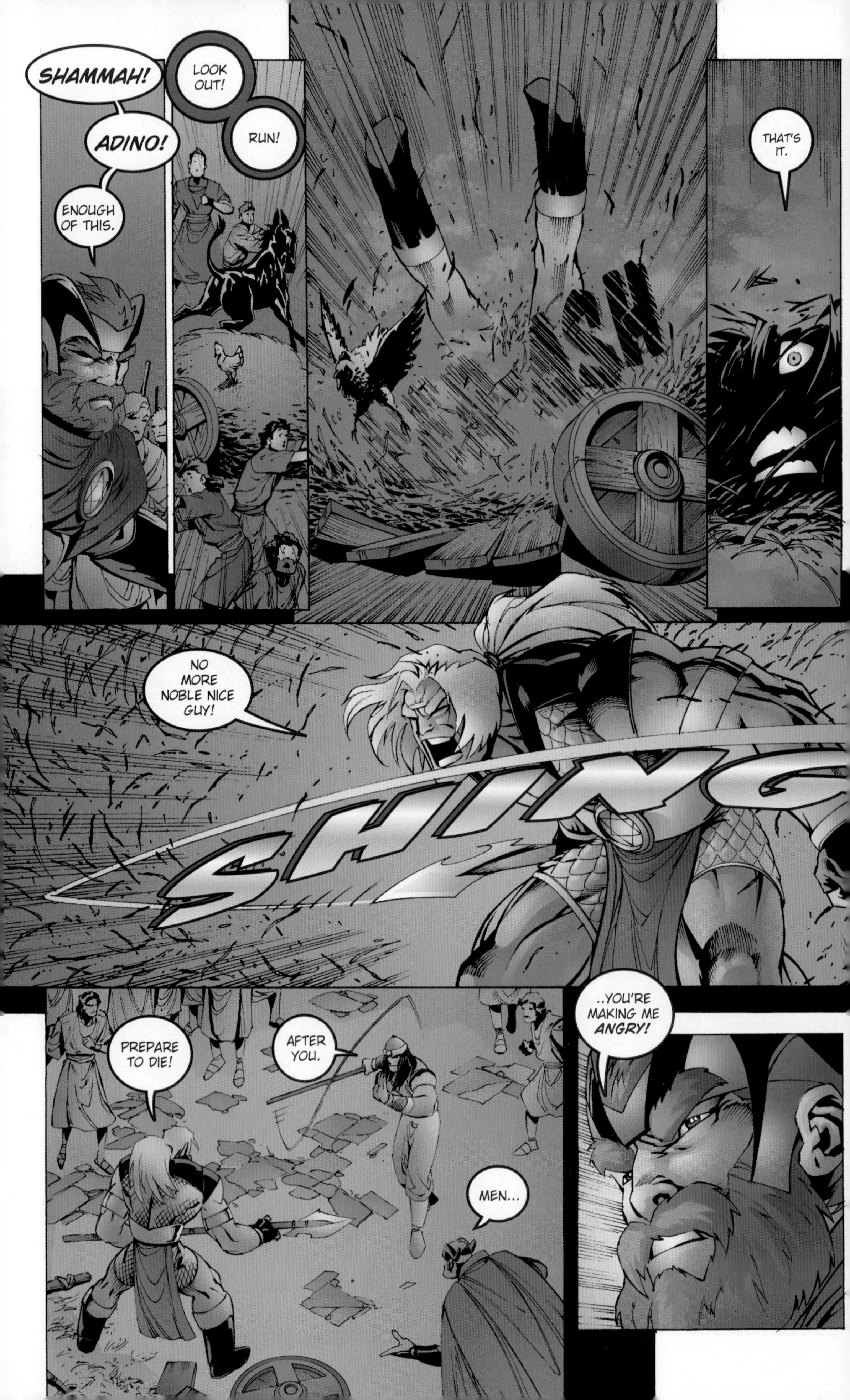
SHAMMAH!
ADINO!
ENOUGH OF THIS.
LOOK OUT!
RUN!
THAT'S IT.
NO MORE NOBLE NICE GUY!
SHING
PREPARE TO DIE!
AFTER YOU.
MEN...
..YOU'RE MAKING ME ANGRY!

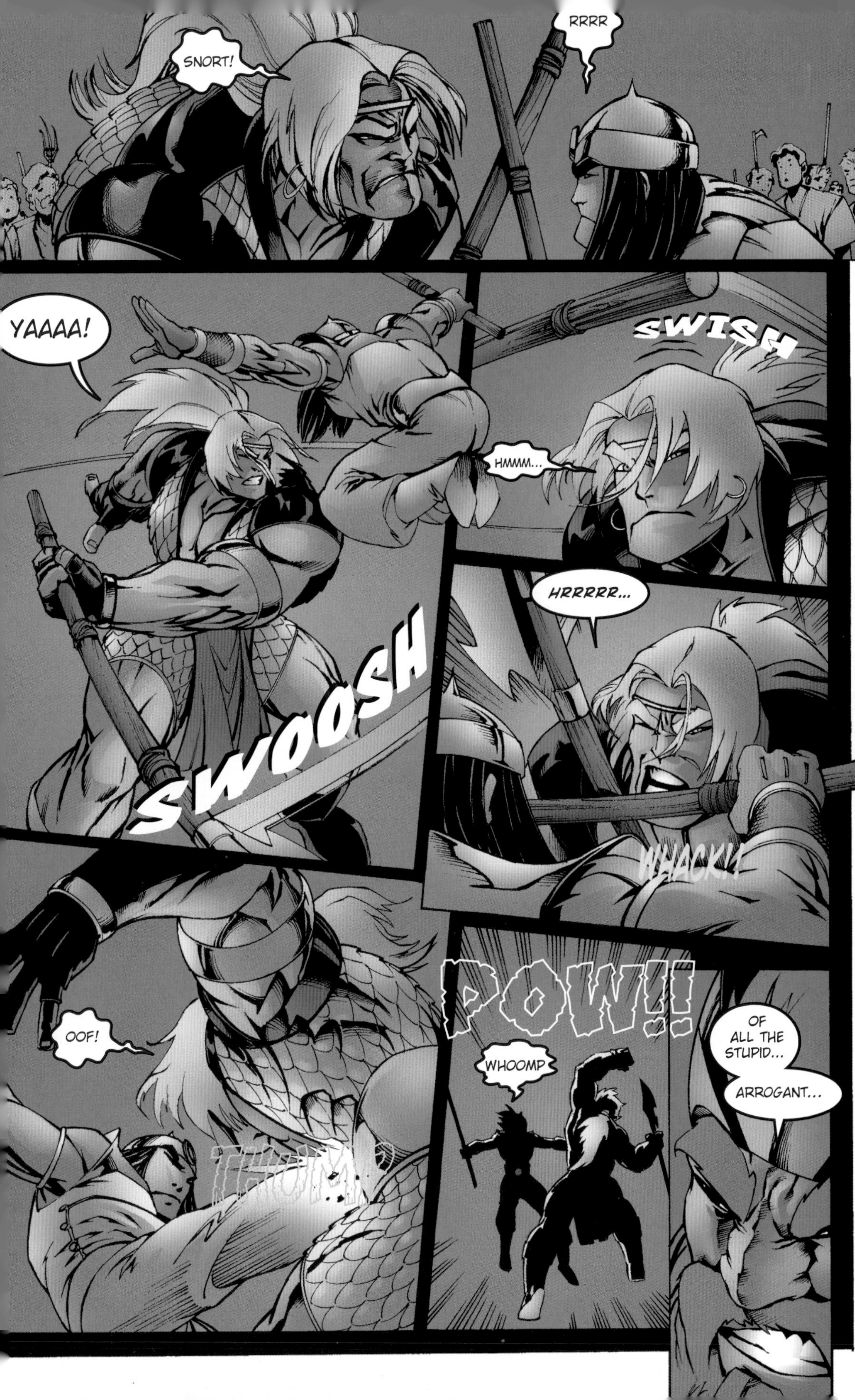
SNORT!
RRRR
YAAAA!
SWOOSH
SWISH
HMMM...
HRRRRR...
WHACK!!
OOF!
POW!!
WHOOMP
OF ALL THE STUPID...
ARROGANT...

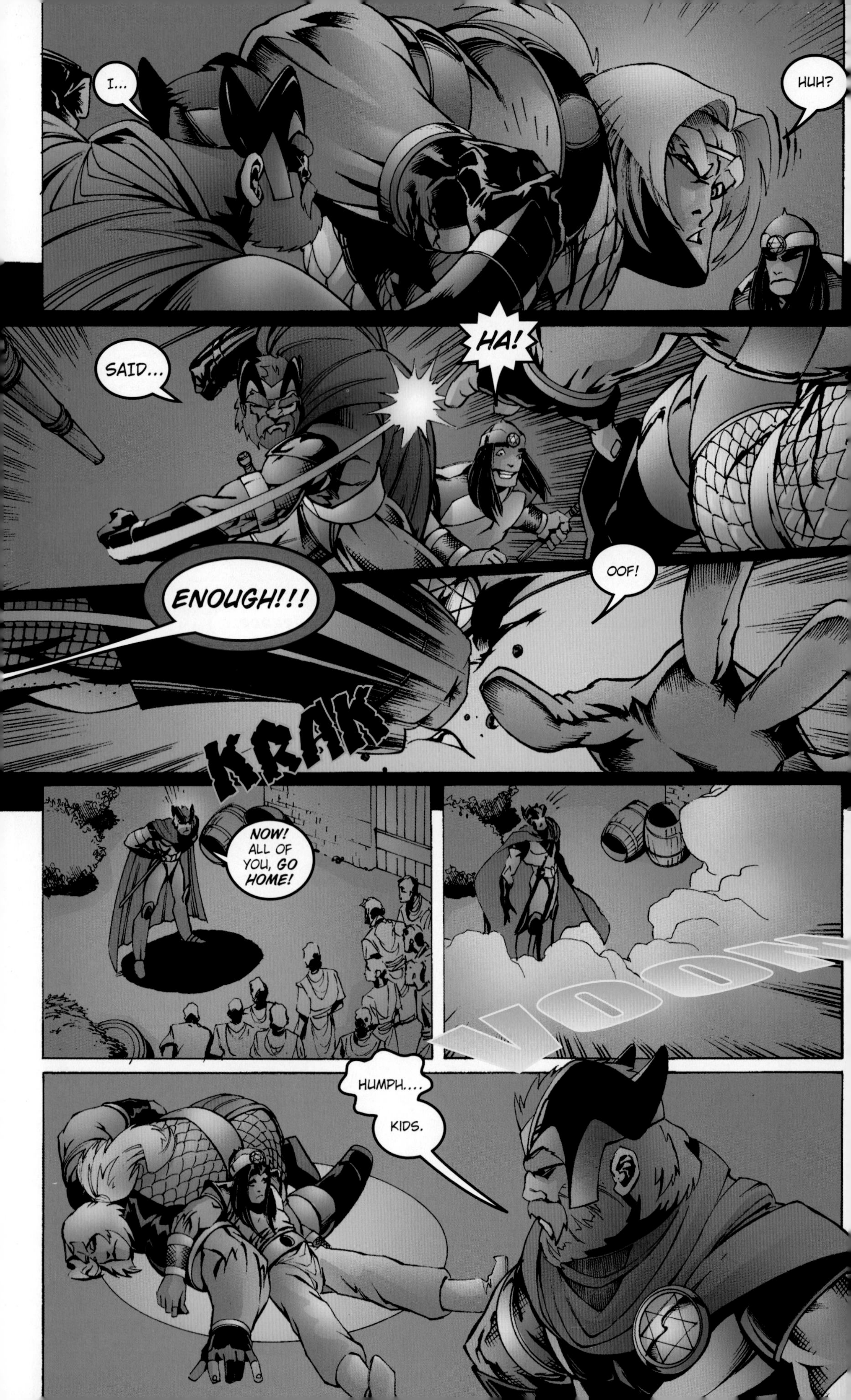
I...
HUH?
SAID...
HA!
ENOUGH!!!
OOF!
KRAK
NOW! ALL OF YOU, GO HOME!
VOOM
HUMPH....
KIDS.

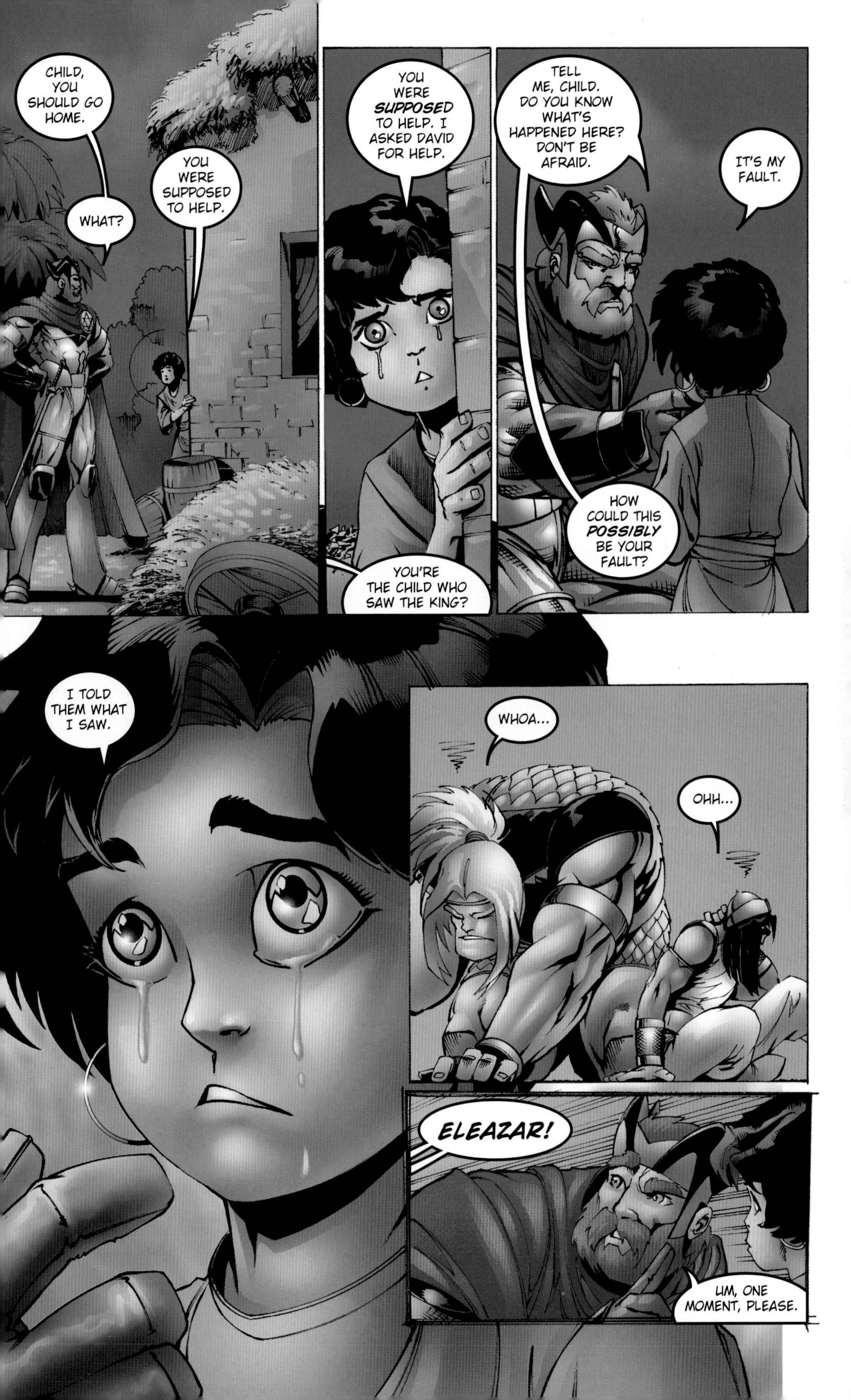
CHILD, YOU SHOULD GO HOME.
WHAT?
YOU WERE SUPPOSED TO HELP.
YOU WERE ***SUPPOSED*** TO HELP. I ASKED DAVID FOR HELP.
YOU'RE THE CHILD WHO SAW THE KING?
TELL ME, CHILD. DO YOU KNOW WHAT'S HAPPENED HERE? DON'T BE AFRAID.
IT'S MY FAULT.
HOW COULD THIS ***POSSIBLY*** BE YOUR FAULT?
I TOLD THEM WHAT I SAW.
WHOA...
OHH...
ELEAZAR!
UM, ONE MOMENT, PLEASE.

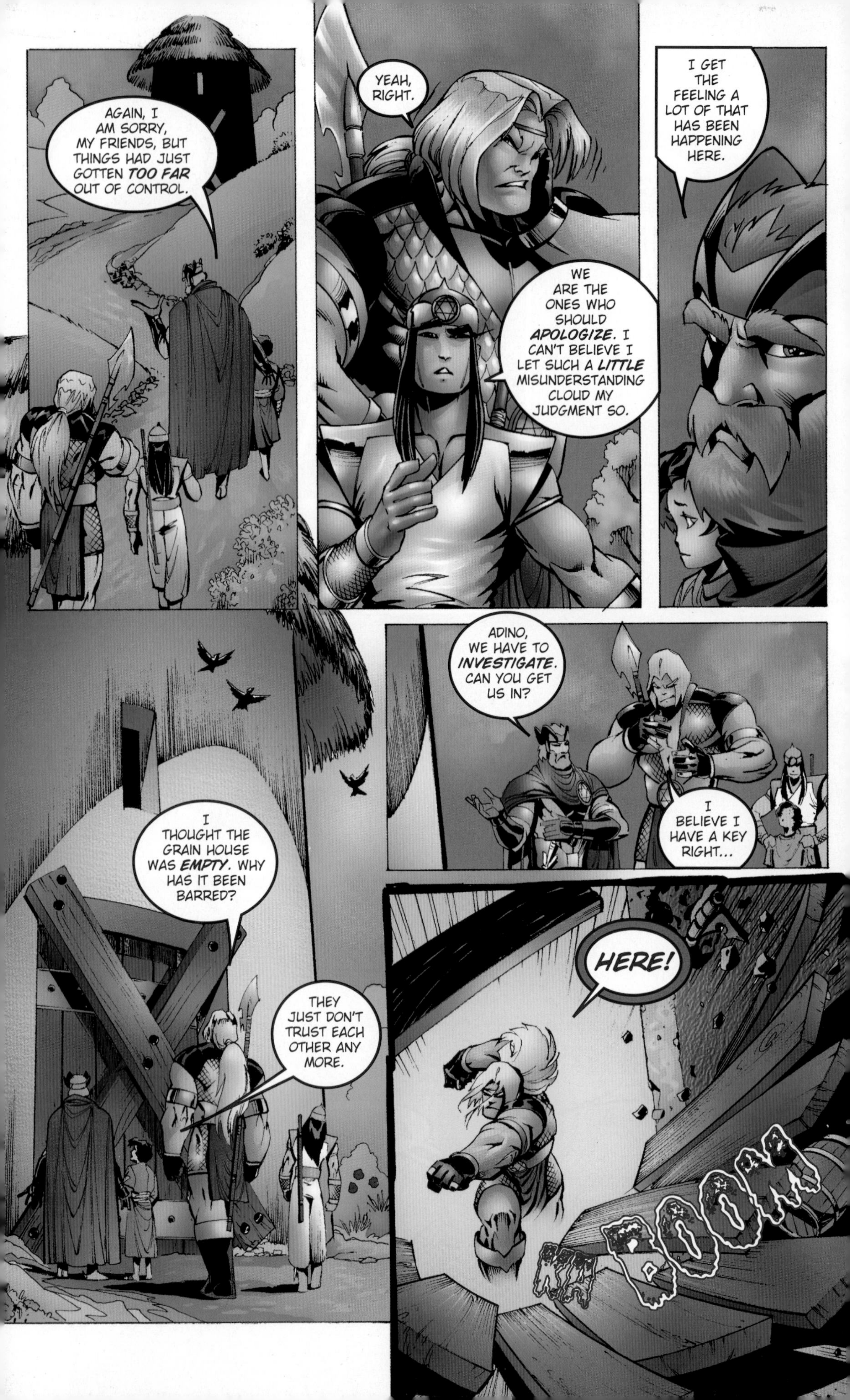
AGAIN, I AM SORRY, MY FRIENDS, BUT THINGS HAD JUST GOTTEN **TOO FAR** OUT OF CONTROL.
YEAH, RIGHT.
WE ARE THE ONES WHO SHOULD **APOLOGIZE**. I CAN'T BELIEVE I LET SUCH A **LITTLE** MISUNDERSTANDING CLOUD MY JUDGMENT SO.
I GET THE FEELING A LOT OF THAT HAS BEEN HAPPENING HERE.
I THOUGHT THE GRAIN HOUSE WAS **EMPTY**. WHY HAS IT BEEN BARRED?
THEY JUST DON'T TRUST EACH OTHER ANY MORE.
ADINO, WE HAVE TO **INVESTIGATE**. CAN YOU GET US IN?
I BELIEVE I HAVE A KEY RIGHT...
HERE!

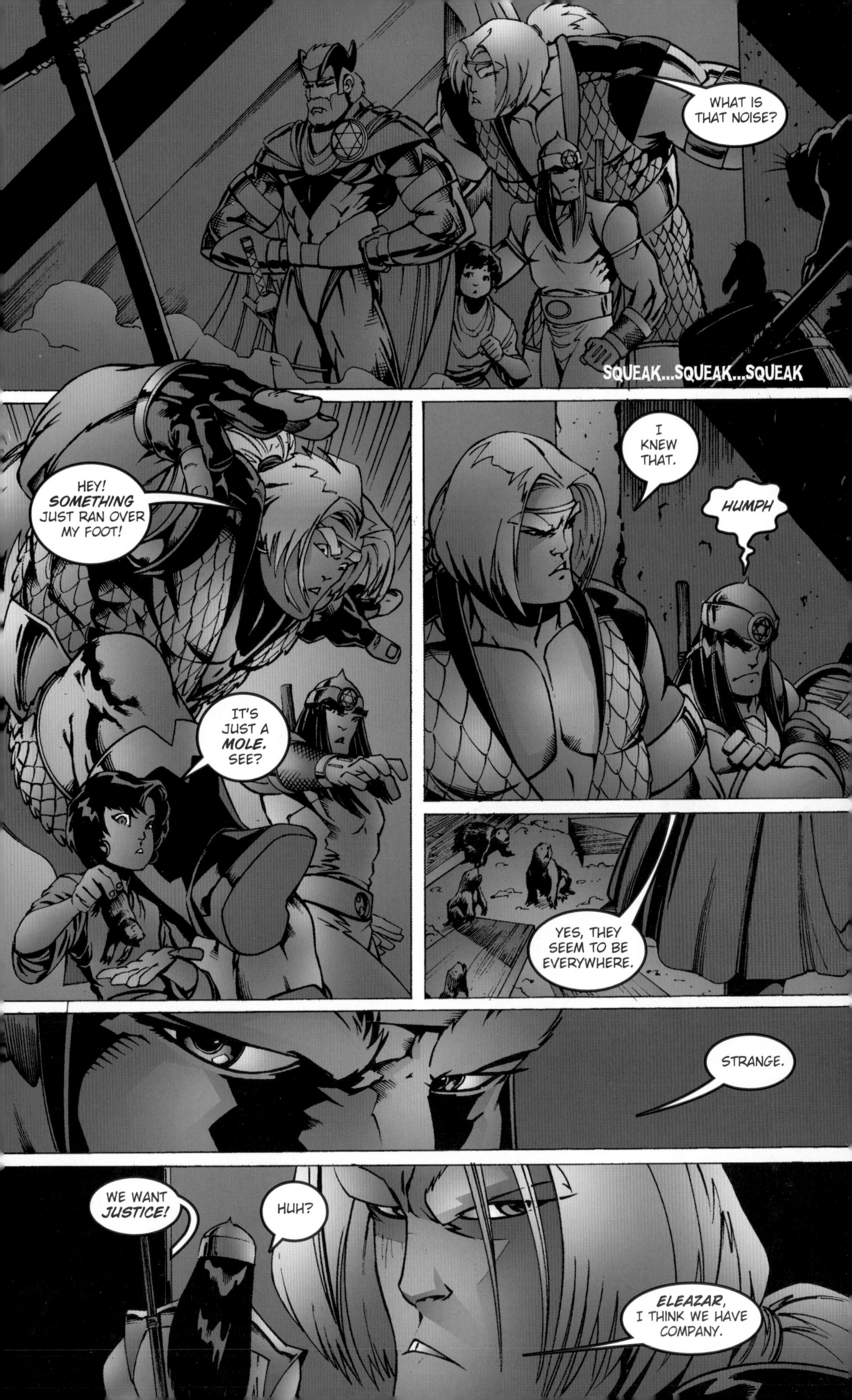
WHAT IS THAT NOISE?
SQUEAK...SQUEAK...SQUEAK
HEY! SOMETHING JUST RAN OVER MY FOOT!
IT'S JUST A MOLE. SEE?
I KNEW THAT.
HUMPH
YES, THEY SEEM TO BE EVERYWHERE.
STRANGE.
WE WANT JUSTICE!
HUH?
ELEAZAR, I THINK WE HAVE COMPANY.

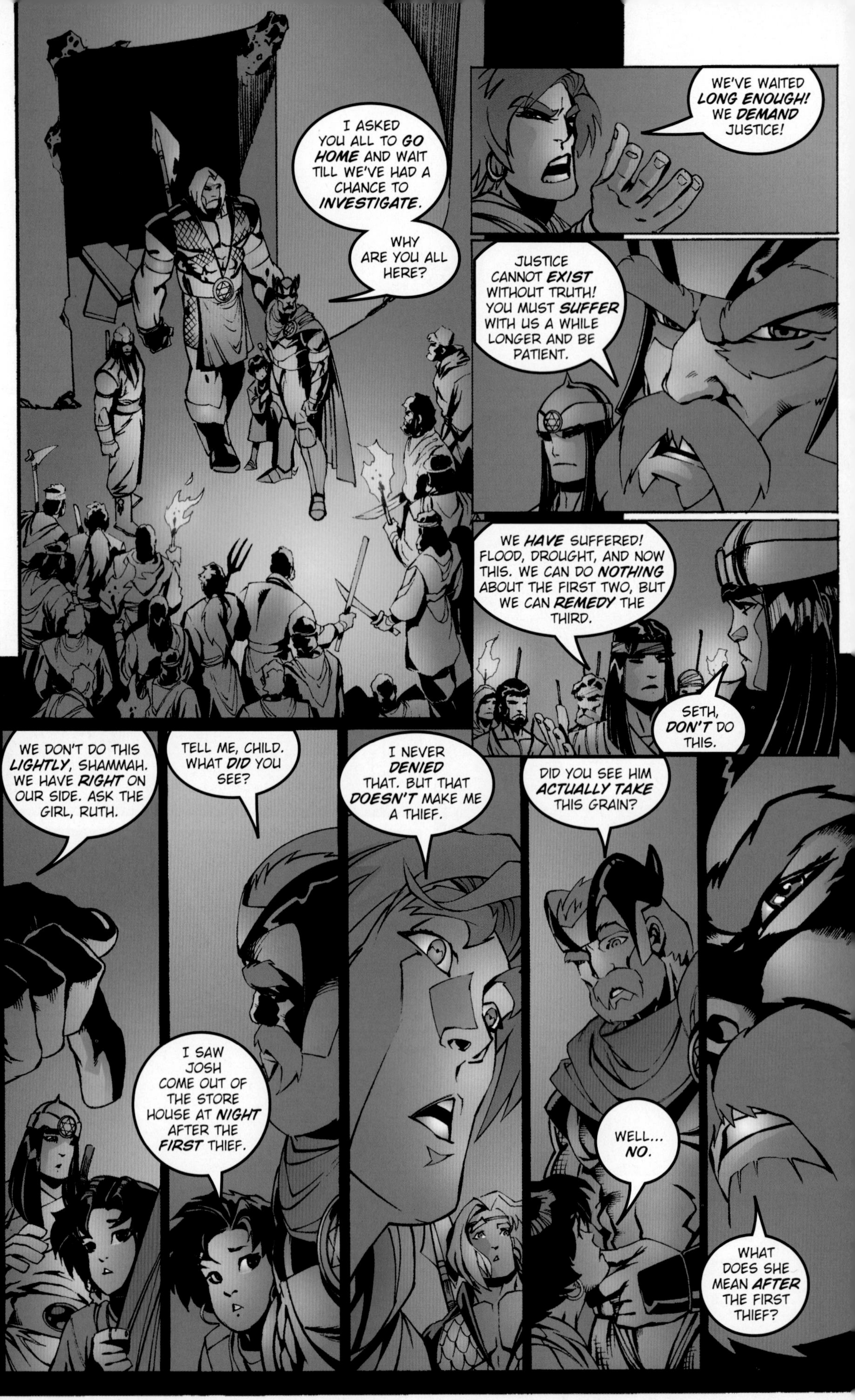
I ASKED YOU ALL TO GO HOME AND WAIT TILL WE'VE HAD A CHANCE TO INVESTIGATE.
WHY ARE YOU ALL HERE?
WE'VE WAITED LONG ENOUGH! WE DEMAND JUSTICE!
JUSTICE CANNOT EXIST WITHOUT TRUTH! YOU MUST SUFFER WITH US A WHILE LONGER AND BE PATIENT.
WE HAVE SUFFERED! FLOOD, DROUGHT, AND NOW THIS. WE CAN DO NOTHING ABOUT THE FIRST TWO, BUT WE CAN REMEDY THE THIRD.
SETH, DON'T DO THIS.
WE DON'T DO THIS LIGHTLY, SHAMMAH. WE HAVE RIGHT ON OUR SIDE. ASK THE GIRL, RUTH.
TELL ME, CHILD. WHAT DID YOU SEE?
I SAW JOSH COME OUT OF THE STORE HOUSE AT NIGHT AFTER THE FIRST THIEF.
I NEVER DENIED THAT. BUT THAT DOESN'T MAKE ME A THIEF.
DID YOU SEE HIM ACTUALLY TAKE THIS GRAIN?
WELL... NO.
WHAT DOES SHE MEAN AFTER THE FIRST THIEF?

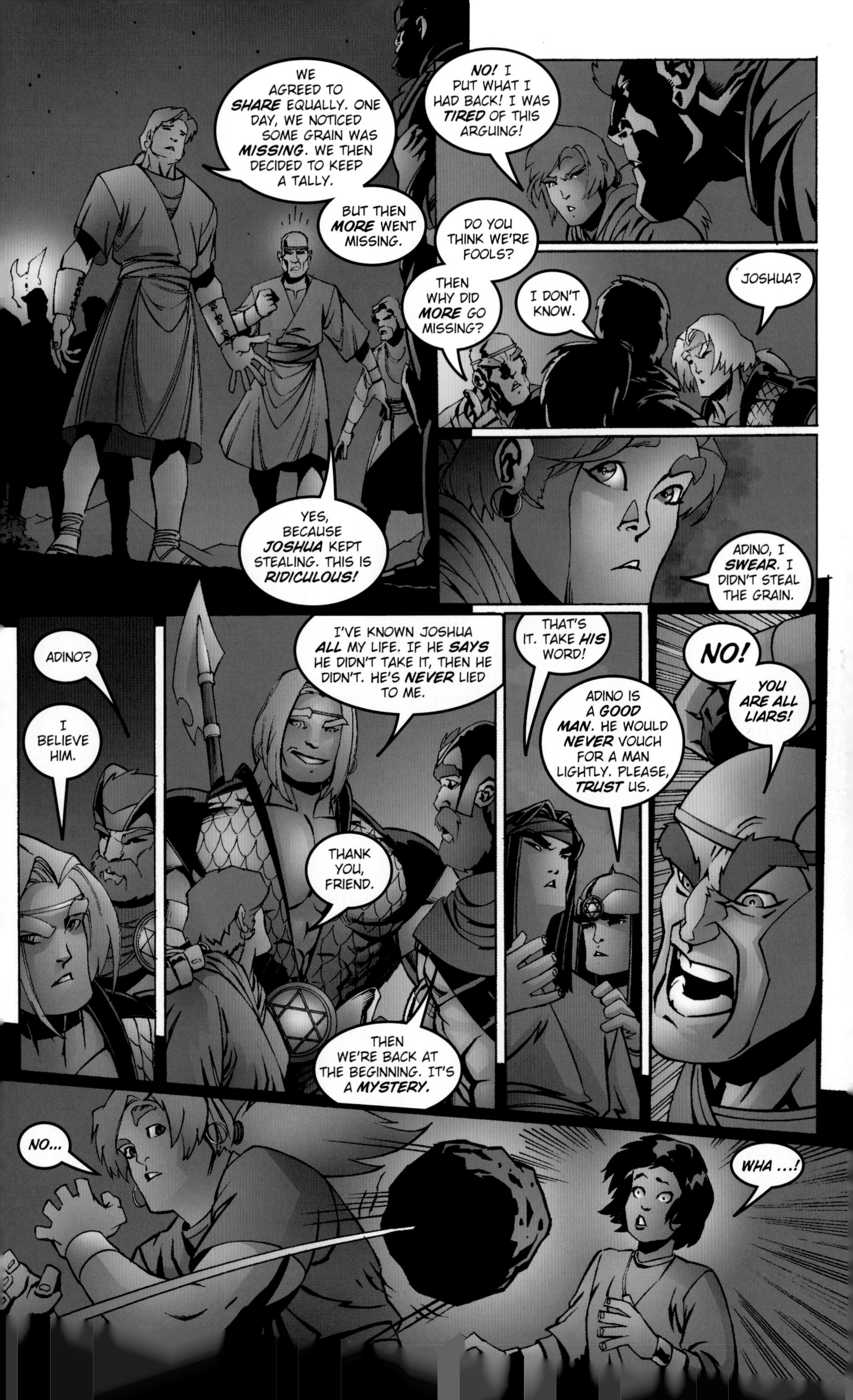
WE AGREED TO **SHARE** EQUALLY. ONE DAY, WE NOTICED SOME GRAIN WAS **MISSING**. WE THEN DECIDED TO KEEP A TALLY.
BUT THEN **MORE** WENT MISSING.
YES, BECAUSE **JOSHUA** KEPT STEALING. THIS IS **RIDICULOUS!**
NO! I PUT WHAT I HAD BACK! I WAS **TIRED** OF THIS ARGUING!
DO YOU THINK WE'RE FOOLS?
THEN WHY DID **MORE** GO MISSING?
I DON'T KNOW.
JOSHUA?
ADINO, I **SWEAR**. I DIDN'T STEAL THE GRAIN.
ADINO?
I BELIEVE HIM.
I'VE KNOWN JOSHUA **ALL** MY LIFE. IF HE **SAYS** HE DIDN'T TAKE IT, THEN HE DIDN'T. HE'S **NEVER** LIED TO ME.
THANK YOU, FRIEND.
THEN WE'RE BACK AT THE BEGINNING. IT'S A **MYSTERY.**
THAT'S IT. TAKE **HIS** WORD!
ADINO IS A **GOOD MAN**. HE WOULD **NEVER** VOUCH FOR A MAN LIGHTLY. PLEASE, **TRUST** US.
NO!
YOU ARE ALL LIARS!
NO...
WHA ...!

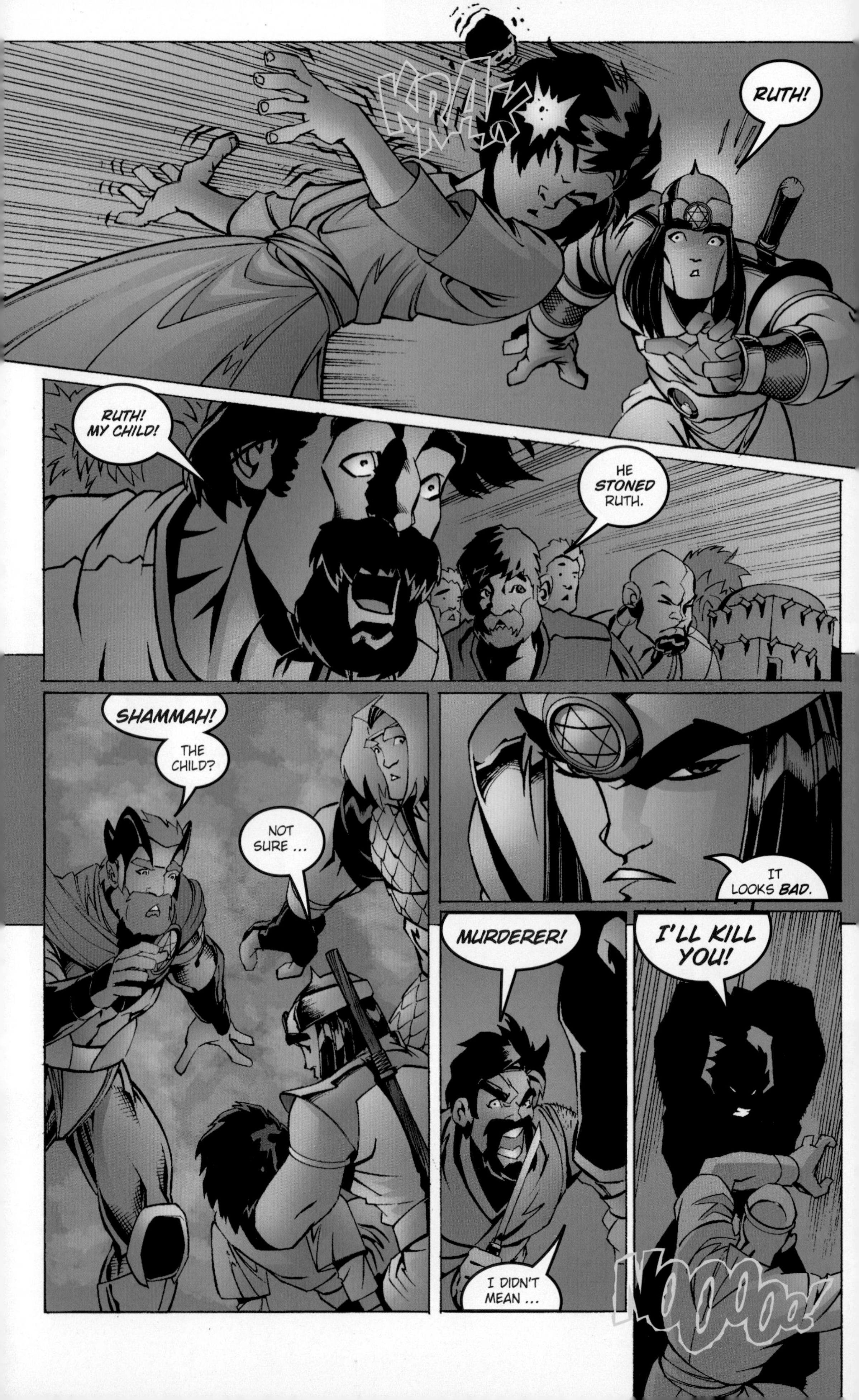
KRAK
RUTH!
RUTH! MY CHILD!
HE STONED RUTH.
SHAMMAH!
THE CHILD?
NOT SURE ...
IT LOOKS BAD.
MURDERER!
I DIDN'T MEAN ...
I'LL KILL YOU!
NOOOO!

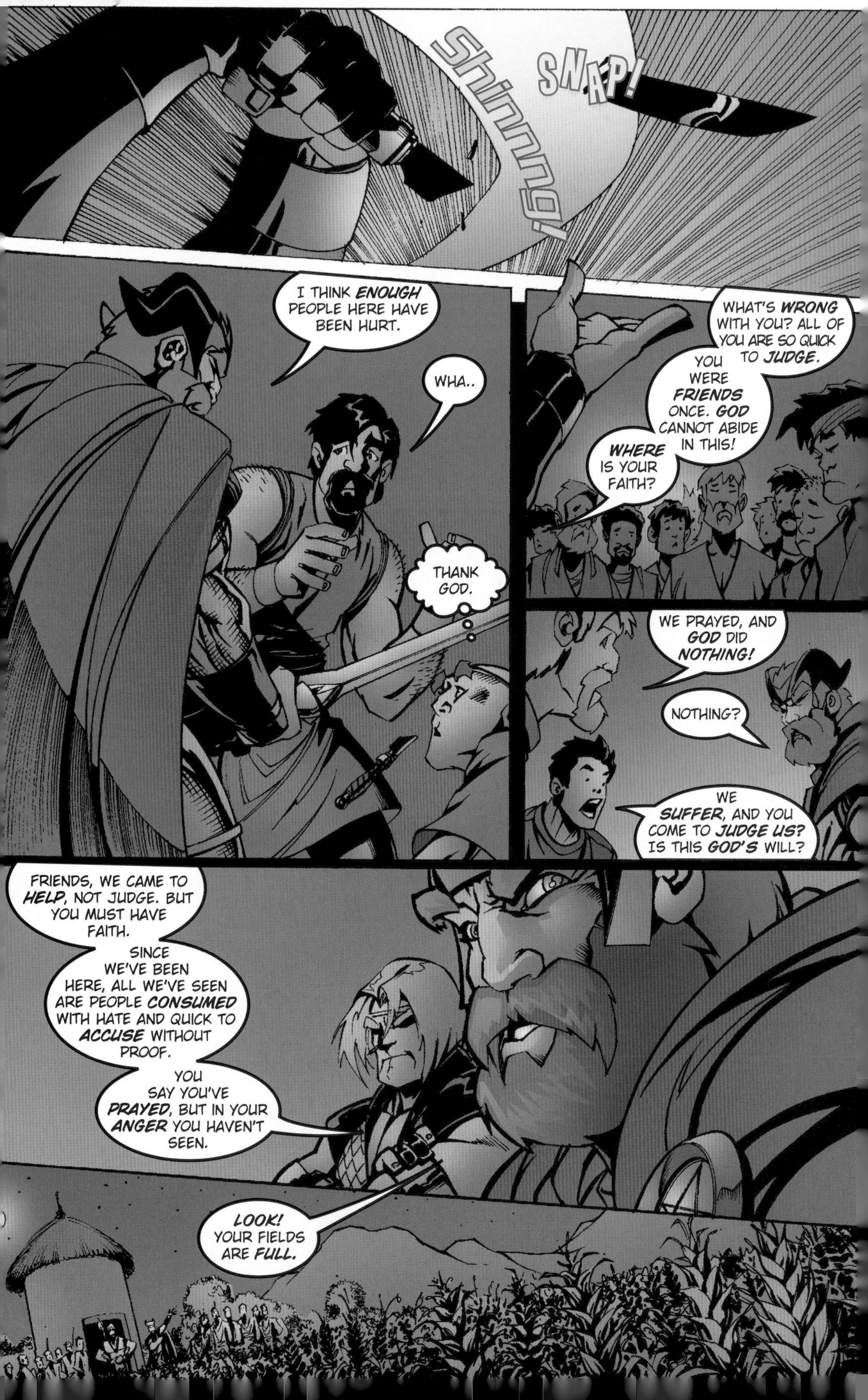
Shinnng!
SNAP!
I THINK ENOUGH PEOPLE HERE HAVE BEEN HURT.
WHA..
THANK GOD.
WHAT'S WRONG WITH YOU? ALL OF YOU ARE SO QUICK TO JUDGE.
YOU WERE FRIENDS ONCE. GOD CANNOT ABIDE IN THIS!
WHERE IS YOUR FAITH?
WE PRAYED, AND GOD DID NOTHING!
NOTHING?
WE SUFFER, AND YOU COME TO JUDGE US? IS THIS GOD'S WILL?
FRIENDS, WE CAME TO HELP, NOT JUDGE. BUT YOU MUST HAVE FAITH.
SINCE WE'VE BEEN HERE, ALL WE'VE SEEN ARE PEOPLE CONSUMED WITH HATE AND QUICK TO ACCUSE WITHOUT PROOF.
YOU SAY YOU'VE PRAYED, BUT IN YOUR ANGER YOU HAVEN'T SEEN.
LOOK! YOUR FIELDS ARE FULL.

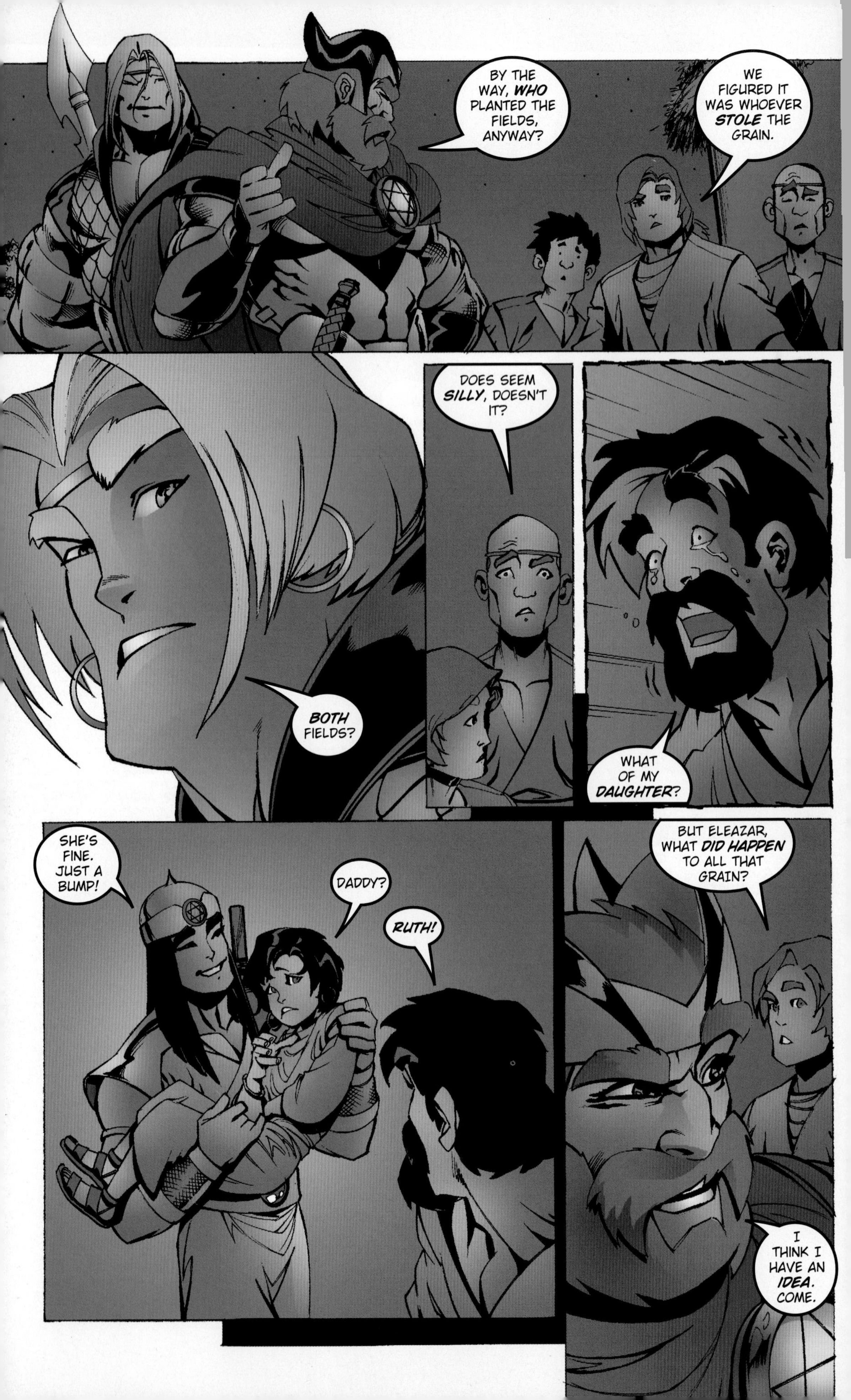
BY THE WAY, **WHO** PLANTED THE FIELDS, ANYWAY?
WE FIGURED IT WAS WHOEVER **STOLE** THE GRAIN.
BOTH FIELDS?
DOES SEEM **SILLY**, DOESN'T IT?
WHAT OF MY **DAUGHTER**?
SHE'S FINE. JUST A BUMP!
DADDY?
RUTH!
BUT ELEAZAR, WHAT **DID HAPPEN** TO ALL THAT GRAIN?
I THINK I HAVE AN **IDEA**. COME.

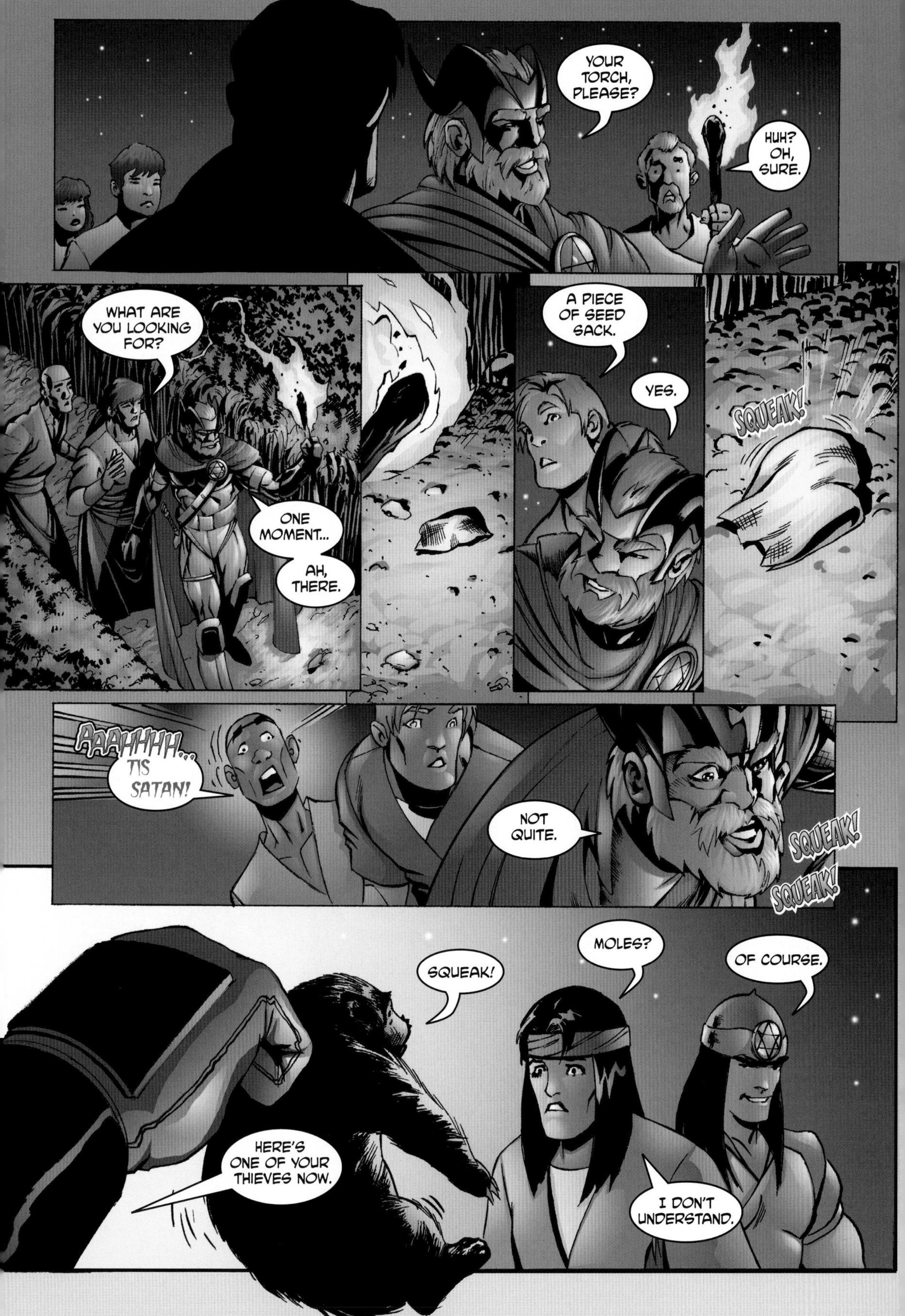
YOUR TORCH, PLEASE?
HUH? OH, SURE.
WHAT ARE YOU LOOKING FOR?
ONE MOMENT...
AH, THERE.
A PIECE OF SEED SACK.
YES.
SQUEAK!
AAAHHHH...
'TIS SATAN!
NOT QUITE.
SQUEAK!
SQUEAK!
SQUEAK!
MOLES?
OF COURSE.
HERE'S ONE OF YOUR THIEVES NOW.
I DON'T UNDERSTAND.

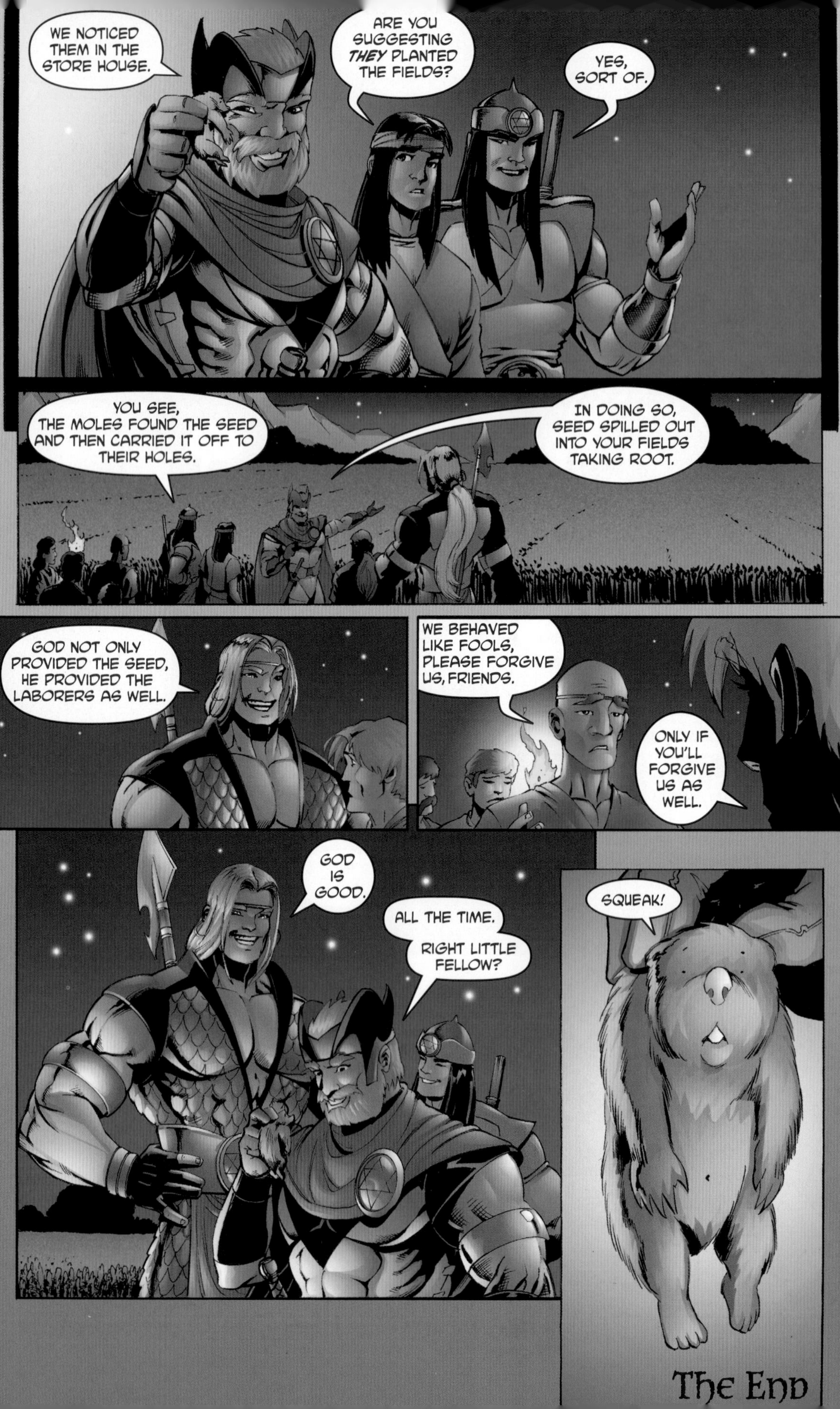
WE NOTICED THEM IN THE STORE HOUSE.
ARE YOU SUGGESTING *THEY* PLANTED THE FIELDS?
YES, SORT OF.
YOU SEE, THE MOLES FOUND THE SEED AND THEN CARRIED IT OFF TO THEIR HOLES.
IN DOING SO, SEED SPILLED OUT INTO YOUR FIELDS TAKING ROOT.
GOD NOT ONLY PROVIDED THE SEED, HE PROVIDED THE LABORERS AS WELL.
WE BEHAVED LIKE FOOLS, PLEASE FORGIVE US, FRIENDS.
ONLY IF YOU'LL FORGIVE US AS WELL.
GOD IS GOOD.
ALL THE TIME.
RIGHT LITTLE FELLOW?
SQUEAK!
The End

SHAMMAH

Name: Shammah, Son of Agee

Height: 5'5"

Weight: 165 lbs

Hair Color: Black

Eye Color: Black

Weapon: The Staff

Reference: II SAM 23:11

Character Description:

"Peaceful as a tempest" best describes this quiet, unassuming little man. Raised to be a priest but destined to be a warrior, Shammah has disciplined both mind and body to a level few have ever dreamed of. A student of scripture and nature, Shammah is a bit of a "know-it-all" at times, but his only desire is to serve God and man as best he can.

ELEAZAR

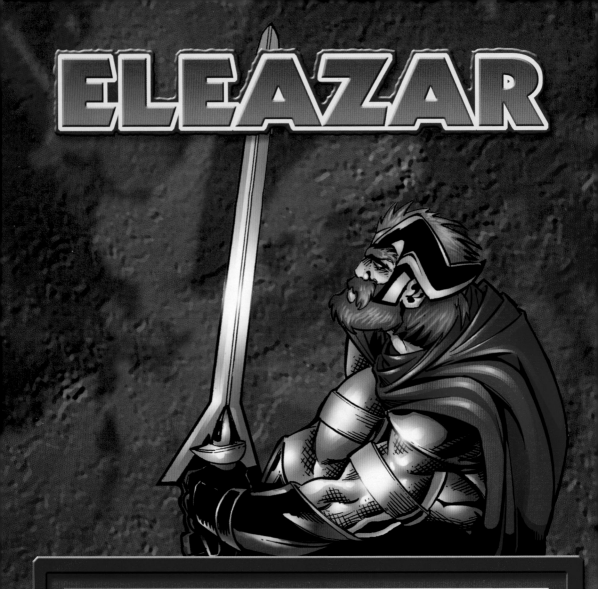

Name: Eleazar, Son of Dodo
Height: 6'1"
Weight: 205 lbs
Hair Color: Red

Eye Color: Green
Weapon: The Sword
Reference: II SAM 23:9

Character Description:

Everything Eleazar has ever gained in life he's earned through hard work and tenacity--including the right to be called a noble. Though he can be overzealous and downright stubborn at times, his motives are always pure. Beneath the rough exterior lies the heart of a man who longs for justice and peace. Eleazar is a godly man with high hopes and deep feelings for God's nation, Israel.

ADINO

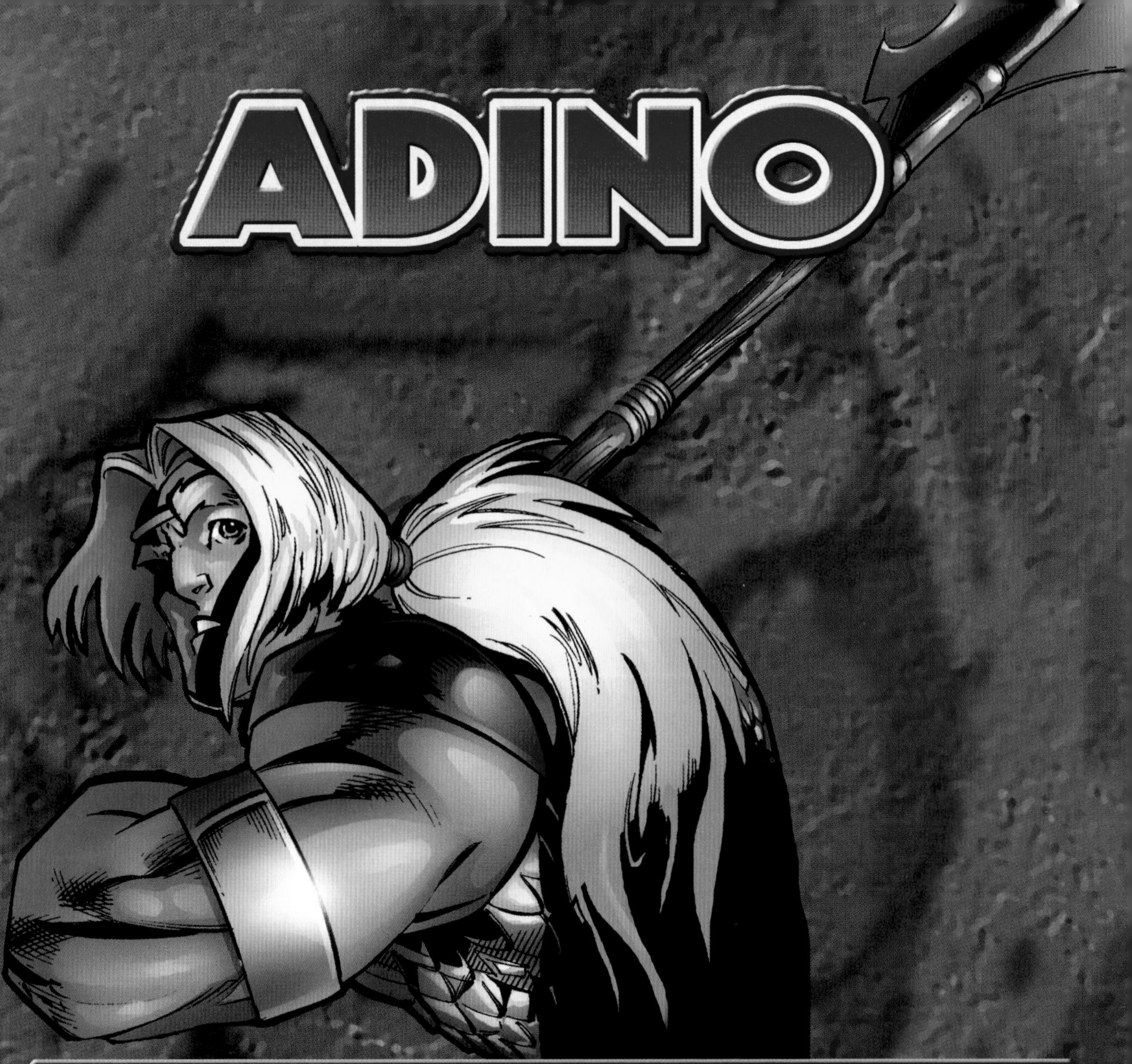

Name: Adino (also "Josheb-Basshebeth"), a Tachemonite
Height: 8'7"
Weight: 320 lbs
Hair Color: Blonde
Eye Color: Blue
Weapon: The Spear
Reference: II SAM 23:8

Character Description:

"Biggest of the Big, Strongest of the Strong!" According to the Gospel of Adino, Adino lives a charmed life. Born of noble blood and blessed with physical prowess and good looks, Adino is the "Golden Boy" supreme. Many would let this sort of thing go to their heads, and so does Adino. Although a bit on the conceited side, Adino has heart and respect for his God and country, and he is a more loyal friend than you could ever find.

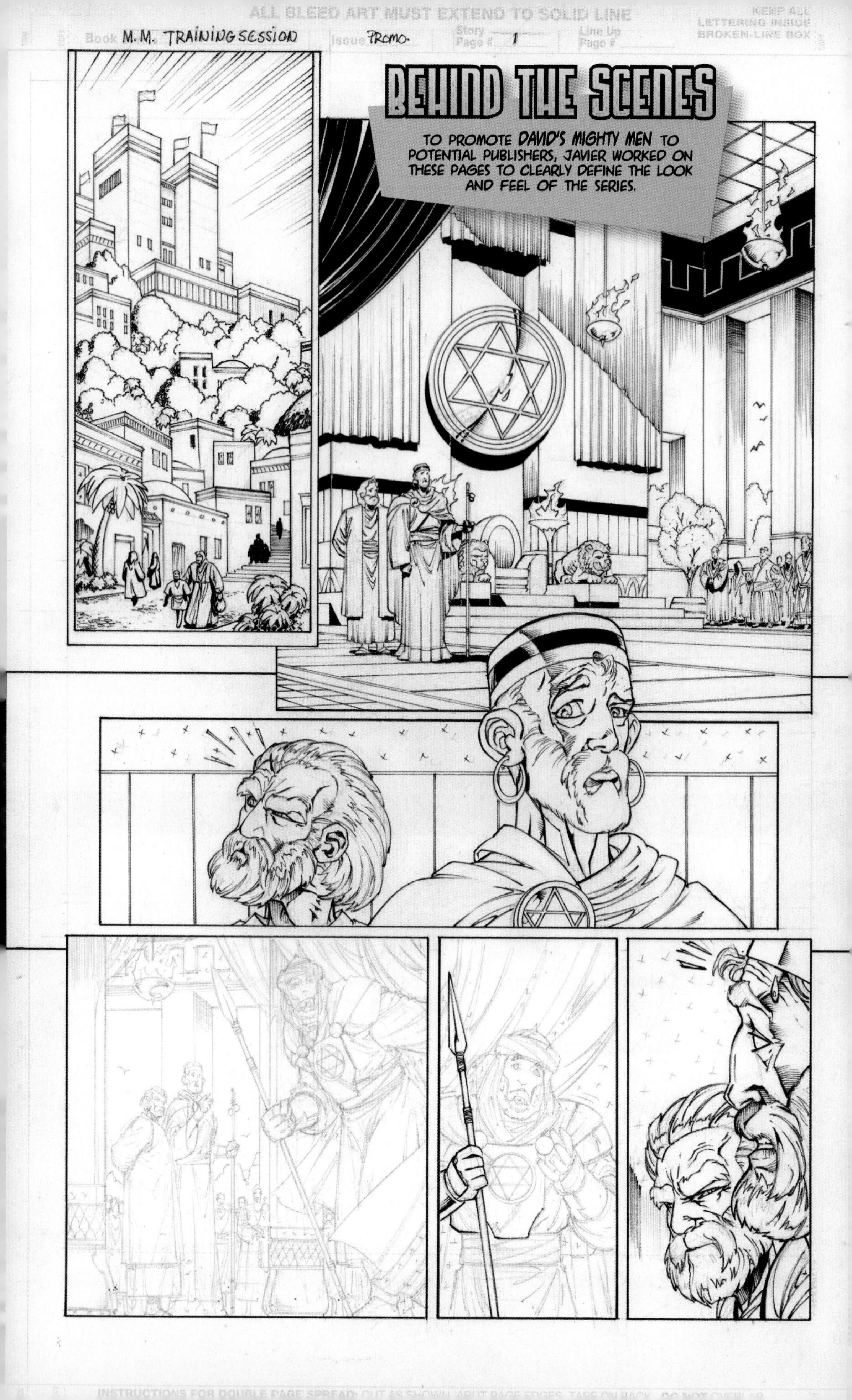
ALL BLEED ART MUST EXTEND TO SOLID LINE
KEEP ALL LETTERING INSIDE BROKEN-LINE BOX
Book M.M. TRAINING SESSION
Issue PROMO.
Story Page # 1
Line Up Page #
INSTRUCTIONS FOR DOUBLE PAGE SPREAD: CUT AS SHOWN, ABUT PAGE EDGES, TAPE ON BACK. DO NOT OVERLAP.

BEHIND THE SCENES

TO PROMOTE *DAVID'S MIGHTY MEN* TO POTENTIAL PUBLISHERS, JAVIER WORKED ON THESE PAGES TO CLEARLY DEFINE THE LOOK AND FEEL OF THE SERIES.

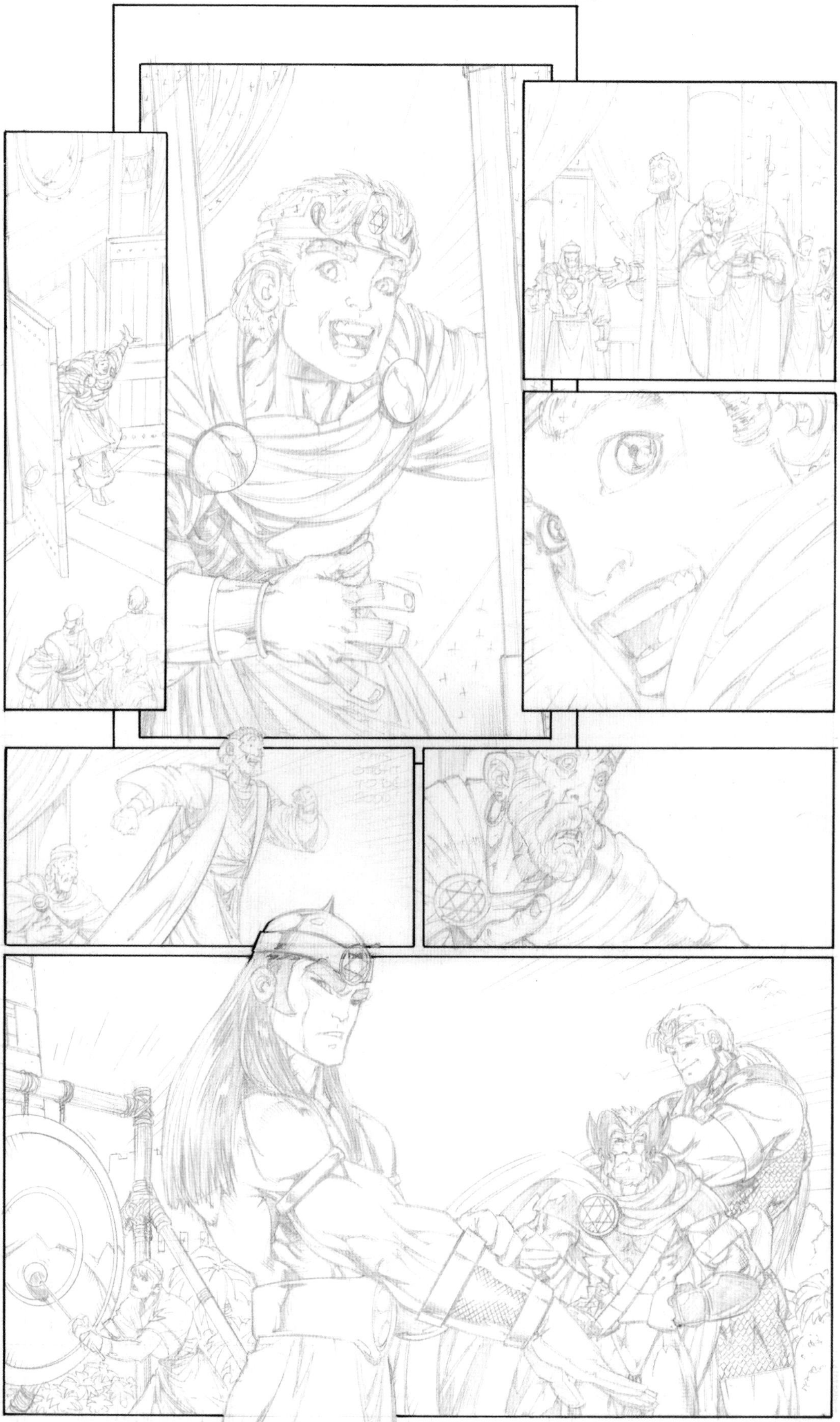

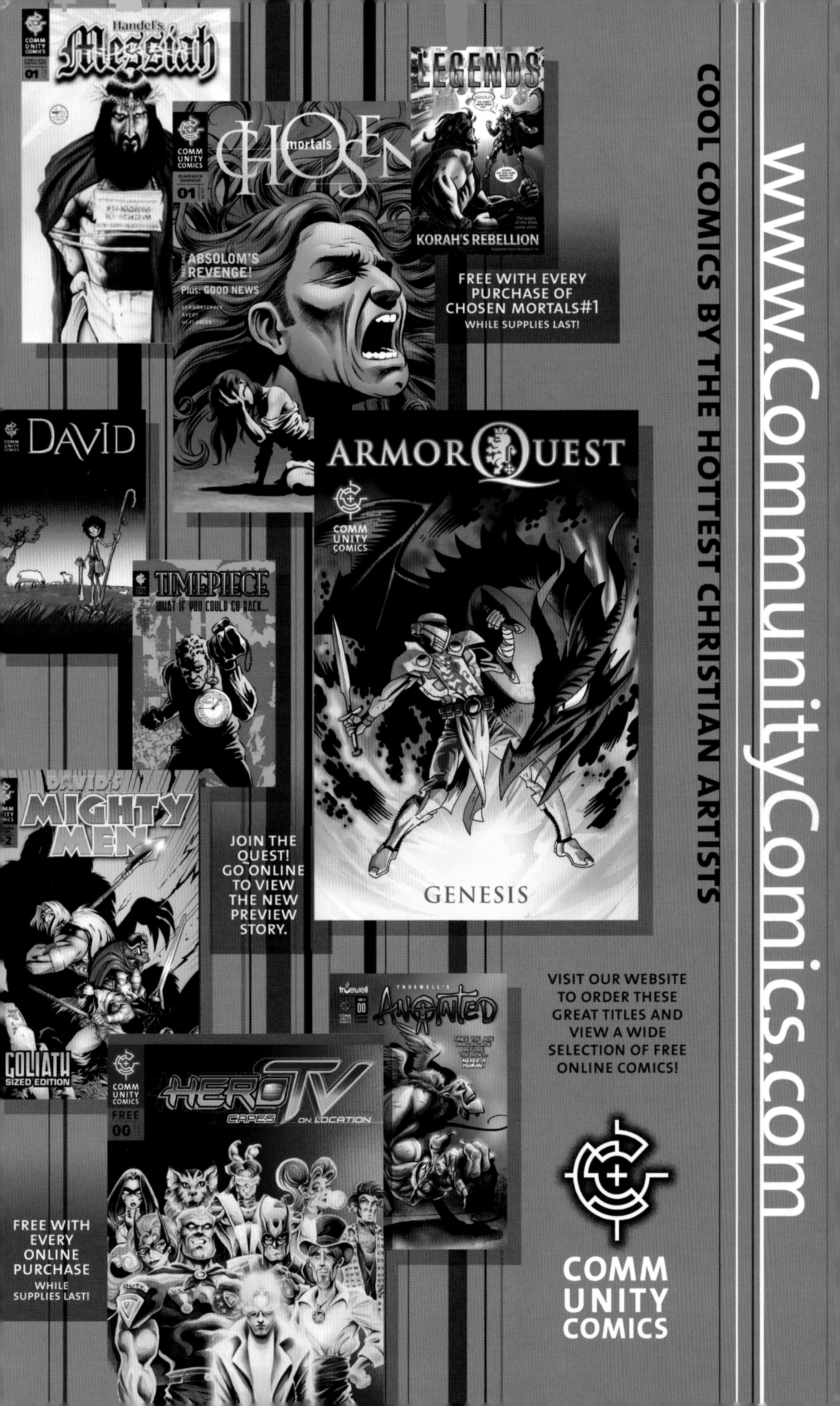
www.CommunityComics.com
COOL COMICS BY THE HOTTEST CHRISTIAN ARTISTS
Handel's Messiah
COMM UNITY COMICS
01
Chosen mortals
01
ABSOLOM'S REVENGE!
Plus: GOOD NEWS
SCHWARTZROCK
AVERY
HI-FI COLOR
LEGENDS
KORAH'S REBELLION
FREE WITH EVERY PURCHASE OF CHOSEN MORTALS#1
WHILE SUPPLIES LAST!
DAVID
TIMEPIECE
WHAT IF YOU COULD GO BACK...
ARMORQUEST
GENESIS
DAVID'S MIGHTY MEN
GOLIATH SIZED EDITION
JOIN THE QUEST! GO ONLINE TO VIEW THE NEW PREVIEW STORY.
TRUEWELL'S ANOINTED
HERO TV
CAPES ON LOCATION
FREE
00
FREE WITH EVERY ONLINE PURCHASE
WHILE SUPPLIES LAST!
VISIT OUR WEBSITE TO ORDER THESE GREAT TITLES AND VIEW A WIDE SELECTION OF FREE ONLINE COMICS!
COMM UNITY COMICS

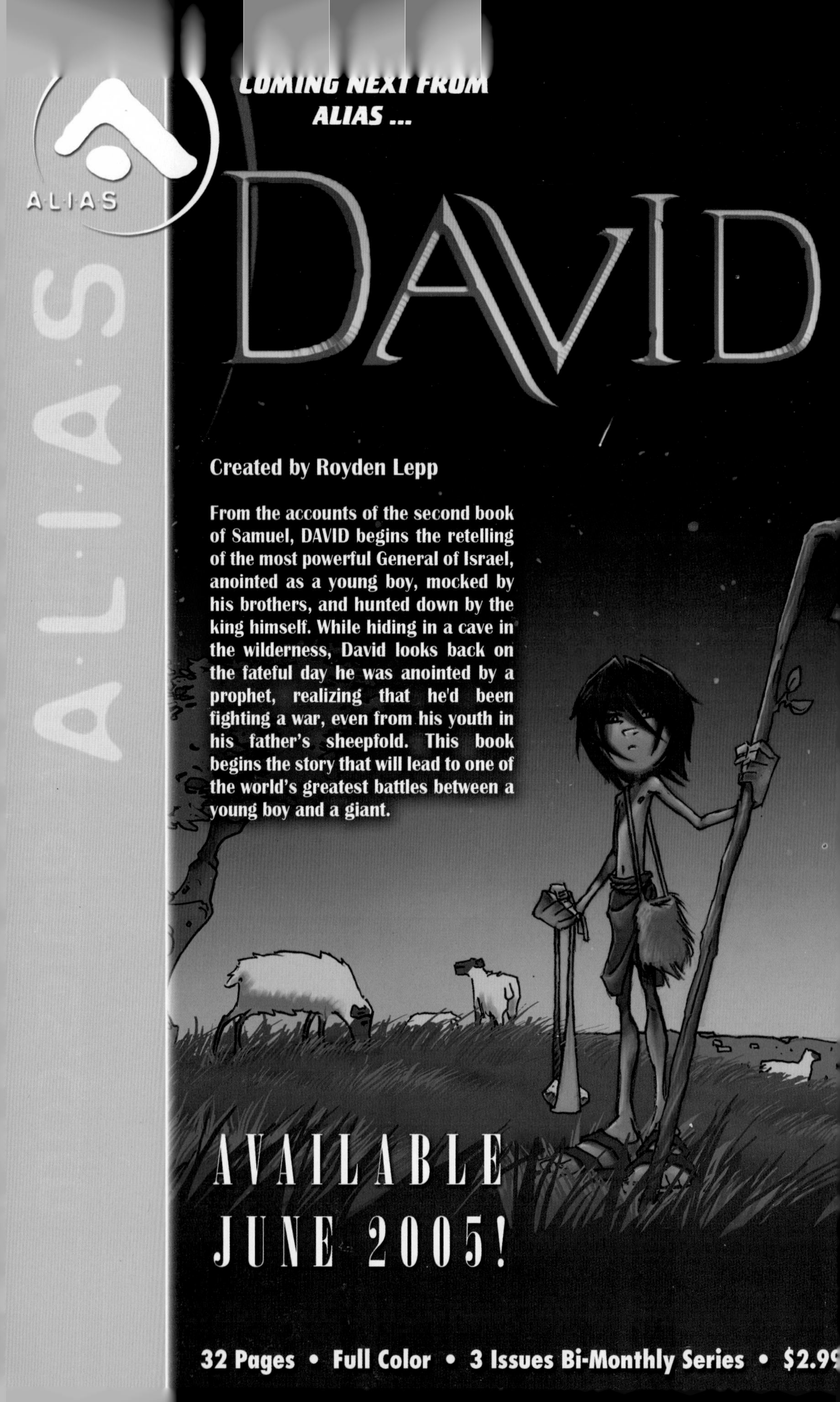
ALIAS
COMING NEXT FROM ALIAS ...
DAVID
Created by Royden Lepp
From the accounts of the second book of Samuel, DAVID begins the retelling of the most powerful General of Israel, anointed as a young boy, mocked by his brothers, and hunted down by the king himself. While hiding in a cave in the wilderness, David looks back on the fateful day he was anointed by a prophet, realizing that he'd been fighting a war, even from his youth in his father's sheepfold. This book begins the story that will lead to one of the world's greatest battles between a young boy and a giant.
AVAILABLE JUNE 2005!
32 Pages • Full Color • 3 Issues Bi-Monthly Series • $2.9
ALIAS